Kathryn Copsey is the project leader of CURBS (Children in URBan Situations) and author of Become Like a Child *(SU, 1994). A trained community worker, she has worked with children for the past 30 years, the majority of which have been in urban situations such as East London. Kathryn is former editor of Scripture Union's SALT programme for 5–7s. She has been part of the authorship team and provided editorial input for all the resources produced under the CURBS umbrella over the past seven years. Kathryn and her husband both live and work in East London and have two grown-up children.*

D1073835

Text copyright © Kathryn Copsey 2005
The author asserts the moral right
to be identified as the author of this work

Published by
The Bible Reading Fellowship
First Floor, Elsfield Hall
15–17 Elsfield Way,
Oxford OX2 8FG
Website: www.brf.org.uk

ISBN 1 84101 386 2
First published 2005
10 9 8 7 6 5 4 3 2 1 0

Acknowledgments
Unless otherwise stated, scripture quotations are taken from the Contemporary English
Version of the Bible published by HarperCollins Publishers, copyright © 1991, 1992,
1995 American Bible Society.

Scriptures quoted from the Good News Bible published by The Bible
Societies/HarperCollins Publishers Ltd, UK © American Bible Society 1966, 1971,
1976, 1992, used with permission.

Scripture quotations taken from the Holy Bible, New International Version, copyright ©
1973, 1978, 1984 by International Bible Society, are used by permission of Hodder &
Stoughton Limited. All rights reserved. 'NIV' is a registered trademark of International
Bible Society. UK trademark number 1448790.

The Living Bible copyright © 1971 by Tyndale House Publishers.

Extracts from the Authorized Version of the Bible (The King James Bible), the rights in
which are vested in the Crown, are reproduced by permission of the Crown's Patentee,
Cambridge University Press.

Seventeen lines from 'Is there a lost child in you?' (p. 63) from *A Tree Full of Angels* by
Macrina Wiederkehr. Copyright © 1988 by Macrina Wiederkehr. Reprinted by
permission of HarperCollins Publishers Inc.

'And these, all these' copyright © Stewart Henderson. Reprinted by permission.

A catalogue record for this book is available from the British Library

Printed in Singapore by Craft Print International Ltd

Understanding the spiritual world of the child

From the ground UP

Kathryn Copsey

'Children are a blessing and a gift from the Lord.'

PSALM 127:3

*For Nigel, whose out-of-the-box thinking,
unwavering encouragement and loving support
have helped visions become realities.*

Acknowledgments

CURBS operates very much as a team. Although I have written this book, many of the insights in it are distilled from the stimulating brainstorming sessions shared with the CURBS Resource Team—Christine Wright, Moira Kleissner and Liz Dorton—as we have met to wrestle with issues and plan new resources. Their creative input and energy has been a constant source of inspiration, and CURBS would not be where it is without them.

This book has also been immeasurably enriched by the work of Keith White. Many years ago, Keith spoke at a conference on marginalization. His visuals were not glossy PowerPoint presentations but illustrations drawn by children. Keith has continually challenged me to start from 'the child in the midst'. I pray that I will always be faithful to that starting point.'

Preface

The CURBS project (Children in URBan Situations) provides support and resources for children's workers in inner cities and on outer urban estates.

The vision for CURBS arose out of many years of working with inner-city children. Running church-based Sunday groups, after-school clubs and holiday clubs for local children highlighted the need for training and support for leaders. It also brought into focus the need for relevant resources—resources that started in the world of the child, rather than assuming levels of literacy, biblical knowledge, types of activities, and patterns of attendance and family life more relevant to suburban middle-class communities. Innovative thinking and new approaches were desperately needed.

CURBS is more than simply a tool or a resource to be dropped into an urban church struggling with its children's work. Underlying the project is a philosophy that challenges traditional approaches to working with children. Within CURBS, children are seen as 'flames to be fanned' rather than 'jugs to be filled'. CURBS is about a different way of working with children, one that starts in the child's world and is about earning the right to be heard, building relationships, and working holistically. To this end, the ethos underlying CURBS marries three important strands of thought and practice:

- **Spirituality:** CURBS takes seriously and works with the belief that children are made in the image of God and therefore have an innate spirituality. Within CURBS we are researching ways in which churches can be encouraged to explore and nurture the spirituality of children.
- **Developmental processes:** CURBS values the insights to be gained from the processes involved in child development and from psychological therapies, and believes that we need consciously to integrate these insights into the way we work with children.

- **Urban context:** CURBS recognizes that urban life presents challenges that are unique in many aspects, and is constantly exploring ways in which we can understand, value and connect with these distinctives.

The seeds of CURBS were planted in East London in the 1970s. Church-linked community work with children indicated that there was a need for Christian resources designed for use with inner-city children, which publishers were not providing. It also showed that there were no groups making provision specifically for the training needs of urban children's workers. Following a pilot project in the early 1980s, supported by a local charity in the London Borough of Newham, the vision finally became a reality in 1996 when the CURBS project was set up as a three-year pilot venture by the Missions and Media Resources departments of Scripture Union.

During these three years, contacts were established, a resource and support team were gathered, a pilot resource kit was produced and evaluated, training modules were developed and further kits were planned. The need for such a project was clearly confirmed. When Scripture Union funding was no longer available, CURBS became a charitable trust in its own right (in 1999), securing funding for the project leader, who became full-time at the end of 2003.

Kathryn Copsey, the current project leader, had the original vision for the project. She ran the pilot venture under Scripture Union and launched CURBS as a charity in 1999. Kathryn has had many years' experience as a community worker with children, coordinating and running after-school and holiday clubs in London. In the 1980s, she undertook a research project that looked at 'the institution of the Sunday school in an inner London borough'. A practical outcome of this research was resource material which later became the basis for a CURBS resource, and the research itself helped to form the theoretical foundation for the project. Kathryn has since continued her training in a number of related areas.

CURBS is supported by a highly committed team of volunteers

who are involved at all levels, from creating, writing and editing the resources, to devising and delivering the training. The project is managed by a steering group, under the guidance of an advisory group, and the work as a whole is overseen by trustees.

Aims, resources and training

The project has two principal aims:

- To provide Christian resources specifically geared to the needs of inner-city children and those on outer urban estates.
- To provide support, training and encouragement for children's workers in such areas, by means of training and resource days, networking and partnerships.

CURBS resources are undated, ungraded, low-cost, photocopiable packs called CURBStone Kits, designed for use mainly with five- to eleven-year-olds. They are primarily issues-based, starting in the child's own world, using themes such as unfairness, self-esteem, friendship and so on to enable children to make links between their world and God's story. The materials reflect the fact that many children are non-readers, so they explore other approaches to learning, such as discovering ways of touching the child's spirituality through the use of imagination and creativity, and through enabling children to explore and value their urban community. Key to the CURBS approach is that it operates on a 'bottom up' model, incorporating the ideas and feedback of users into subsequent kits as far as is possible. The CURBS team is also exploring the possibility of acting as a 'clearing house' to produce and circulate locally written resources. Kits are produced as and when funding is available.

The training offered has one or more of the following aspects at its heart: children's spirituality, developmental issues, and the urban context. Around these, CURBS has developed a number of flexible modules such as 'Understanding children's spirituality', 'Valuing and listening to children' and 'Challenging children'. CURBS encourages requests for training that originate from within churches or groups themselves. The team believes in empowering leaders to discover the gifts they have within themselves, so an appropriate training package is then planned in conjunction with individual churches or groups. CURBS also encourages groups of churches to work together, as such an approach helps to foster co-operation and networking at a local level.

CURBS follows an issues-based approach to training, so that leaders are encouraged to think through their approach to children's work rather than simply to pick up practical skills.

Partnership and networking

CURBS is committed to working on a partnership model, acknowledging that the kingdom of God can best be furthered by pooling resources and ideas, and recognizing the richness of approach and the breaking down of barriers that can happen when groups and individuals work to a common goal. For example, the Christmas resource *Unwrapping Christmas* was produced jointly with Unlock, a national organization working with urban adults. CURBS is also working with BRF, with a view to publishing some of the CURBS resources once the initial print run has sold out.

In addition, CURBS maintains ongoing contacts with various denominational groups, diocesan children's advisors, those responsible for supporting workers in urban priority areas, and groups such as Unlock, Frontier Youth Trust, Scripture Union Scotland, the Evangelical Coalition for Urban Mission, and other organizations with an urban remit.

The team has also established a good working relationship with Netherne Printing Services, who print all the resources. They are a part of Surrey Oaklands Mental Health Trust and retrain people with disabilities for integration back into the wider community. This link is mutually beneficial and in keeping with the CURBS ethos of working with the most marginalized in society.

There are currently nearly 800 individuals and churches on the CURBS mailing list, the majority of whom have used the materials and/or been involved in training, or have attended conferences in which CURBS has been involved. The users are located throughout England, Scotland and Ireland, and the resources have even been used in translation in parts of eastern Europe. An interesting and unexpected group of users consists of those from rural areas faced, like urban users, with small groups of children, a wide age-range, and limited resources in terms of both personnel and equipment. The undated, ungraded nature of the resources, together with the low cost, meets a real need for such a group.

Contents

Foreword

Kathryn Copsey invites us to join her on a spiritual journey. She is a sensitive and empathetic companion who is still travelling, and this book represents her reflections before she moves on. The children and young people among whom she works will not allow her thoughts to become set or fossilized into neat frameworks or formulations.

It is a journey to the margins of our social world and consciousness, where children in poor urban settings become the focus of our attention. However, we look through their eyes rather than at them.

It is a journey within our own spirits and souls as Kathryn leads by example, sharing some very personal feelings and experiences that have moulded her personality and identity.

It is a journey in the company of some of the wisest writers on children and their development, including Janusz Korczak, Alice Miller, Eric Berne, Sofia Cavaletti, Lev Vygotsky, and more recently Robert Coles, David Hay, Rebecca Nye, Jerome Berryman, Glenn Miles, Jo Wright, Marcia Bunge, Dawn Devries and Catherine Stonehouse.

It is a journey that visits territories and academic disciplines usually kept apart, so that a philosophy of childhood enriched by Christian wisdom and professional insights begins to emerge.

It is a journey where the little child—an unsentimentalized version named David, Sam, Jamie, Natalie, Kyle, Cassie, Ben—leads us as adults, so that we can 'see' them and receive them as they are.

It is a journey where the footprints of Jesus can be traced, fresh at every junction and turn.

It is a journey that Jesus calls us to undertake if we are to enter the kingdom of heaven.

Surprisingly few Christian leaders and theologians have heard the call of Jesus to follow him by allowing the child in the midst to cast new light on our understanding of the kingdom of heaven. Kathryn

12

has written a practical book that those working alongside children and young people will treasure, but that also has the potential to open eyes and hearts of all Christians to some hidden truths of the gospel.

Keith White
Director, Mill Grove
Trustee of the Child Theology Movement and the Christian Child Care Forum

Beginning the story

This week, I listened to a sermon based around the parable of the lost son—or, to set the focus correctly, the parable of the loving father. The speaker set out to look at the qualities of the father in the story and to show how they paralleled the qualities we can see in God as Father. 'Right,' I thought. 'I've got the sermon tied up! Let's see... forgiveness, probably, and a willingness to accept us no matter what we've done; then maybe a gentle rebuke around jealousy and self-righteousness. Good stuff—although I've heard it before many times in one form or another.'

How wrong I was! There was no mention of forgiveness or acceptance, no mention of repentance or jealousy. Three aspects of God's love for us were brought out. First of all, God holds us in his thoughts; we are constantly on his mind. The father had no idea when his son would return, but he must have been continually hovering on his doorstep, longing and watching, because one day he spied his son when he was still just a dot in the distance. Second, God values us. Although the son had gone off and done his own thing, in his father's eyes he was still as precious as he had ever been. Third, God celebrates us. The father called for a ring and robe and sandals. He prepared a great party. He wasn't celebrating anything his son had done; he was celebrating him for who he was, for the joy of having him home.

This sermon helped me to enter the parable in a new way because it connected with my feelings, both in being a parent myself and in remembering my parents. It moved beyond theological concepts such as forgiveness, acceptance and repentance: as important as these may be, they are nevertheless abstract. They are also the usual concepts we hear about when we unpack the parable. (Perhaps because of this, they do not help us to connect with the powerful impact of the parable at a 'feeling' level.) Instead, the sermon approached the parable from a different perspective. I know what it is like to hold my children in my thoughts, in my heart. I know how important it is for my children to know that they are remembered even when they are far away. I remember what it is to be valued myself, to be loved and prayed for every day by my parents. I know how that knowledge has held me in many difficult situations. I know what it is to celebrate my own children for who they are. I recall the many parties we celebrated together year by year as they grew up.

These truths, as applied to God, gave the parable new meaning because they connected with my feelings—not just with my head. Let's be honest, most of us can probably sit through a traditional sermon on this parable thinking, 'Yes, it is wonderful to know that God accepts me when I come to him in repentance and that he will forgive all that I have done wrong.' We can leave church having heard again a talk on wonderful truths of salvation (another concept!) but at what point has it touched our feelings? At what point does it make a difference to the way we see and experience the world?

I have used this illustration because, for me, it explains exactly what I have tried to do in this book. Having trained as a community worker and spent over 30 years working with children in one capacity or another, I am well used to all the language, concepts and approaches we draw upon when working with children. What are children like at different ages... what is child protection all about... what are good ways of helping children to worship... how do we draw families into our churches... what is the value of adventure play... what about children and death or divorce... what about children and competitive games... how do we encourage children to pray...? The list is endless. All of these are very important issues and need to be explored, but it often feels that these issues are *about* children.

Having my own children and working with children in play-groups, in church, in holiday clubs, in after-school clubs and in community centres brings me face-to-face with children. They enter my world and touch it. They touch my feelings. They touch who I am and they change me. I realized that I wanted more than just to think *about* children. That seemed very superficial. Instead I wanted to 'become like a child' and to experience the world from their perspective. I needed to develop a child-centred attitude. I needed to understand and explain what was happening at a much deeper level, and for this I found that I needed the insights of particular psychological therapies. However, as far as I am aware, not much has been written that attempts to fuse a biblical perspective and understanding of the child with the research and insights drawn from psychology and child therapy, anchored firmly within a hands-on experience of working with children.[1] That is the aim of this book.

I stumbled into children's work by default: 'We think you can do it… There's no one else…' Sound familiar? Many years and many levels of training later, I still often wonder if I can do it, but by now I have discovered that I don't have to be an expert. What children need from me is to be 'good enough', and to be present and genuine in my relationships with them. Perhaps the following pages gain their authenticity from the fact that they are not the result of academic learning which I have then sought to put into practice. Rather, they come out of my own personal experiences, 'from the ground up'. God has used my own journey as a child, and sub-sequently as a parent and children's worker, as material for learning and growth. As a result of what I experienced as a child, I learned to shut down, to put on a mask to protect myself, to keep my various worlds separate. I have sought as a parent to do things differently, and I have spent much of my adult life seeking to bring to churches a different way of seeing and of being with children. My passion therefore comes out of my own personal journey.

I have been challenged to look for answers in all sorts of places, from my own childhood, my own children, people I have met, books I have read and studied, places I have visited, and training I have undertaken. Thus, the insights in this book have started with practical application, and only then have I looked for a theory to help in understanding it. In this sense, it is a work in progress, because tomorrow I will have new experiences with children and will be looking for new understandings. I like to think of myself as a reflective practitioner, and I know that many of you reading this book are just the same, so I invite you to share the journey with me and, most especially, in the company of the children you know.

Children are not the people of tomorrow,
But are people of today.
They have a right to be taken seriously,
And to be treated with tenderness and respect.
They should be allowed to grow into whoever they were meant to be—
'The unknown person' inside each of them
is our hope for the future.[2]

About this book

In seeking to fulfil our aims of resourcing, training and supporting urban children's workers, the CURBS model of working with children has a threefold focus—developmental issues, children's spirituality and the urban context—and looks at the intersections between these three factors. Relationships are a key feature in each of these areas. It has been our experience that where relationships in the broadest sense break down, the child's spirituality becomes damaged, and this damage impairs the ability of the child to experience and come to faith. We need first to work with and repair a child's damaged spirituality so that it can be used as a springboard to faith. We believe that this model is unique, in that it has evolved as a result of reflecting on hands-on work with children in the inner city. In other words, it has started in the world of the child and has been developed 'from the ground up'. Connections have then been made with insights drawn from a biblical perspective on the child, community development approaches and psychological therapies, including child therapy, all of which have provided fascinating links and insights.

As we unpack the many themes contained in this model, we begin in the first section with the child him- or herself. We look first at the nature of the child's spirituality, what it means to be made in God's image. Then we step sideways and look at the way in which the child develops and the innate 'hungers'—the developmental needs—that must be met in order for the child to develop into a healthy individual. We see how a life script is developed through the messages taken in from the world around, and how the perception of these messages is affected by the child's experiences. From this we see how the child's spirituality—the inherent image of God— inevitably becomes damaged.

We begin the next section by exploring the biblical perspective on children, including the upside-down values that Jesus demonstrated. The importance of a child-centred attitude is highlighted, before we explore ways of repairing a child's damaged spirituality by drawing on the insights from some psychological therapies. We look at the key role of relationship throughout, and the important role of the 'healthy village' in raising the healthy child. We see how this may be applied in the context of the local church.

The final section attempts to earth the discussion further by setting it in an urban context. We look first at some of the factors that constitute 'the urban', and at Sam, a typical urban child. We then explore how we can connect with Sam, putting in place the cement and bricks that are needed, in order effectively to repair and nurture Sam's damaged spirituality, and help him or her to come to a place where s/he not only feels 'seen' and valued by us as children's workers, but most importantly by God.

NOTES

1   The work of Sofia Cavaletti on the Catechesis of the Good Shepherd, which she developed with Gianna Gobbi, a Montessori educator, wherein adults and children aged three to six dwell together in the mystery of God, draws on an understanding of children through the insights of the Montessori approach to education. See Sofia Cavaletti, *The Religious Potential of the Child* (Catechesis of the Good Shepherd Publications, 1992). See also the work of Jerome Berryman, *Godly Play: An Imaginative Approach to Religious Education* (Augsburg, 1991), which is also grounded in a Montessori approach, and David Hay and Rebecca Nye, *The Spirit of the Child* (Fount, 1998), which draws on psychological perspectives. I would argue, however, that none of these draw on the insights of the psychological therapies.

More recently, Keith White has been drawing together his wide range of childcare experience with his speaking and writing, particularly in the areas of sociology and childcare. In his paper to the Annual Conference of the Christian Child Care Forum, 11 February, 2004, he said, 'There is the glimpse of the possibility of an integration of professional and Christian concepts and perspectives in child development. Jo Wright and I have begun to do some work on this, and you will find the preliminary findings in *Celebrating Children*. What I have been doing over a period of twenty or so years, while engaged in caring for children and young people, is to summarize and crystallize the essential insights of child care theorists such as Piaget, Erikson, Klein, Winnicott, Rutter and many others with a view to seeing what they had in common.' See also his chapters in *Celebrating Children*, Glen Miles and Josephine-Joy Wright, eds. (Paternoster, 2003).

2   Sandra Joseph (ed.), Theresa Prout and Anne Hargest Gorzelak (trans.), *A Voice for the Child: The Inspirational Words of Janusz Korczak* (HarperCollins, 1999), p. 4.

Made in God's image

PART ONE

The spiritual child

From earliest childhood my life has been shot through with God.
MACRINA WIEDERKEHR[1]

When I was a child in Japan, we took our summer holidays in the mountains. I would get on my bike and ride through the forest paths for hours, smelling green smells, feeling the wind in my hair and relishing the space and freedom. I *knew* that around the next corner I would discover a secret waterfall or rare animal never before seen by human eyes. Our early trips to Japan were by ocean liner. I discovered that if I stood on deck at the very stern of the ship and looked out to sea, I did not see the ship at all. There was just the churning wake streaming out to the endless horizon... and me—no one else in the whole world. I imagined I was being present at creation.

Then there was the music. Growing up in a home full of music, I would shut my eyes to the last movement of Saint-Saens' Symphony No 3, hear its rippling phrases and picture the angels busy tidying up heaven before God came striding through to the bold, clean chords that followed.

Are these just childhood imaginings—thoughts and actions that we leave behind when we grow up? Or are they about a childhood 'shot through with God'? In what sense were these experiences about God?

Other adults also seem to identify that children bring some unique and distinct insights and experiences to the world. Henri Nouwen spent time alongside children in Peru.

The children always challenge me to live in the present. They want me to be with them here and now, and they find it hard to understand that I might have other things to do or think about… I marvel at their ability to be fully present to me. Their uninhibited expression of affection and their willingness to receive it pull me directly into the moment and invite me to celebrate life where it is found.[2]

In a wonderfully descriptive passage from her book, *An American Childhood*, Annie Dillard recounts her childhood experience of lying in bed at night, watching the beams of passing headlights travel across her room—only, for her as a child, they were not car headlights. They were far more sinister.

I lay alone and was almost asleep when the damned thing entered the room by flattening itself against the open door and sliding in. It was a transparent, luminous oblong. I could see the door whiten at its touch; I could see the blue wall turn pale where it raced over it… It was a swift spirit; it was an awareness. It made noise. It had two joined parts, a head and a tail, like a Chinese dragon… I dared not blink or breathe; I tried to hush my whooping blood. If it found another awareness it would destroy it. Every night before it got to me it gave up. It hit my wall's corner and couldn't get past. It shrank completely into itself and vanished like a cobra down a hole. I heard the rising roar it made when it died or left. I still couldn't breathe. I knew—it was the worst fact I knew, a very hard fact— that it would return again alive that same night.[3]

Haven't we all, as children, made up stories about things that happen to us every day? How does a child come by the gift of being able to turn a humdrum, everyday event into a story—a story complete with drama, suspense, fear, anticipation?

In *A Tree Full of Angels*, Sr Macrina Wiederkehr tells the story of William Blake, as a child, seeing the rays of the sun shimmering through the branches of a tree, turning the dazzling leaves into the wings of angels. 'Being yet a mere child he was not inhibited about his vision and ran quickly to tell his parents the joyful tidings. "I saw a tree filled with angels."'[4]

My own experiences as a child, reading the experiences of others, and being alongside my own children and children in my groups as they have grown and developed, have convinced me that if we do but look for it, every childhood is shot through with God.

In God's image

This conviction is reinforced by my reading of Genesis 1:26: God said, 'Now we will make humans, and they will be like us.' This verse is not referring to a physical resemblance in terms of flesh and blood, so it follows that God has made us spiritual beings like himself—we all have a spiritual dimension. Our lives are shot through with God. What an amazing fact! Do we fully understand its implications? It means that each child we work with—even the most troubled child—is created in God's image and has spiritual qualities akin to those of God. In other words, each child has an innate spirituality. It is not just when a child begins to take an interest in and respond to Christian teaching that he or she suddenly develops spiritual qualities: they are within the child from the moment of conception.

An awareness of this fact must surely totally transform our attitude to our children. It must mean that we approach them with reverence. This may seem an odd word to use about children, but 'reverence' carries a sense of awe and respect. We are treading on holy ground because, in these children, we are approaching God. In the New Testament, Jesus reinforces this idea: 'And when you welcome one of these children because of me, you welcome me' (Matthew 18:5). Maybe you've been part of a 'march for Jesus' with the aim of 'bringing Jesus' to a town. You may have heard speakers challenging you to 'bring God to these children'. We seem to have failed to recognize that God is already there and active. We need to open our eyes and see where he is at work.

So we recognize that being created in the image of God means that we have a spiritual dimension, a spirituality within us. Let us unpack this theme. How does it manifest itself? How is it different from faith? Take a moment to brainstorm the word 'spirituality'. What are the images and words that come to mind? Here are a few, suggested by various groups of children's workers.

vulnerability	New Age	relationship
experience	well-being	peace
mystical	honesty	inner self
spirit	inwards	feelings
meditation	nature	being in touch with God
prayer	depth	individual
Holy Spirit	death	identity

Pause, and now brainstorm the words and images that you associate with 'faith'.

trust	God	cross	creed
love	truth	home	miracles
hope	a gift	security	Holy Spirit
relationship	family	identity	conflict
obedience	Jesus	crutch	belief
personal			

It may be seen that, while some words are common to both groups, words associated with 'spirituality' tend to relate to notions of 'otherness'—the numinous, qualities of awareness and mystery. Words associated with faith, on the other hand, appear to be more secure and grounded in the sense of confidence, and are linked with the beliefs and practices of a given religious community.

We look later in this section at the categories of 'hungers' with which the child comes into the world. These are basic needs, which must be met if the child is to develop into a healthy, whole individual. While they are expressed as psychological and emotional needs, each also has a physiological basis. Spirituality is not on the list, but clearly warrants inclusion in its own right. We have seen in Genesis the biblical evidence that a spiritual dimension is inborn in each human being. The idea that it also has a biological basis was put forward by the zoologist Alistair Hardy. He speaks of a '"religious experience" [that] has evolved through the process of natural selection because it has survival value to the individual'.[5] In their book *The Spirit of the Child*, David Hay and Rebecca Nye suggest that Hardy's use of the term 'religious experience' is parallel to the term 'spiritual awareness'. 'What he is saying is that there is a form of awareness, different from and transcending everyday awareness which is potentially present in all human beings and which has a positive function in enabling individuals to survive in their natural environments.'[6]

With reference to children, then, I would suggest that a useful starting point is to understand spirituality as 'an innate sensitivity to matters beyond and yet within everyday life'.[7]

We have seen that spirituality is innate or inborn, part of the humanness of each child. We have also seen that it is a 'sensitivity'. It has a numinous quality; it is an awareness that operates at the affective rather than cognitive level—that is, at a feeling response or gut level rather than at a carefully reasoned-out head level. Yet, for children, it is not something 'precious', something to be treated with kid gloves. It is earthy and integrated. Children do not make the distinctions that we make, as adults, between what is sacred and what is secular, the holy and the profane. They do not have a Sunday box and a weekday box. They are holistic and integrated in their approach to life. I recall a father telling me of a shopping trip with his small daughter. As he wheeled her through the supermarket in a trolley, she suddenly stood up, lifted her hands and shouted out, 'Praise the Lord!' Dad had obviously neglected to tell her that the supermarket was not the place to shout such things.

Spirituality is the birthright of each child. David Hay goes on to point out that 'on Hardy's thesis, spirituality is not the exclusive property of one religion, or for that matter of religion in general'.[8] Spirituality is the given for each child, and around this spirituality is built the framework of faith, where faith is the belief, commitment and actions that arise out of a person's spirituality. Faith gives a structure, as it were, to a person's spirituality. So, depending on where and among whom a child is brought up, we will find the faith framework of Islam, of Judaism, of Buddhism, of Christianity, placed around the child's spirituality. If we look at the findings of Robert Coles (and the experience of many of the children with whom we work), we will see that it is also possible to put a secular or even atheistic framework around spirituality.[9] As Christians, our belief is that our spirituality reaches its fullest expression when a Christian framework is applied—when the original image of God imprinted in each person is consciously recognized and responded to in Jesus Christ.

Unpacking spirituality

How do we identify the essence of this spirituality within the child? What are the qualities that are naturally present within the child and go to make up inborn spirituality? Jack Priestly, former principal of Westhill College, once said that to identify spirituality is like telling a child to take a jar, go outside and catch some wind and bring it back in. How do we know there is air in the jar? We cannot see it, touch it or smell it. Spirituality is similarly hard to capture.

Many years ago, I had the privilege of running an after-school club for five- to eleven-year-olds each afternoon for two hours. It often didn't feel like a privilege at the time! However, some years later I sat down and made a list of all the qualities that endeared those children to me, which mean that even now, 30 years later, I still recall some names and incidents. I discovered wonderful gifts in these children: a sense of adventure, spontaneity, imagination, gentleness, joy and wonder in small things, candour, trust, resilience, innocence, giving hearts... the list could go on. And then it clicked! These qualities were what the child's spirituality was all about—not mystical experiences, but very ordinary, everyday living. When Jesus encourages us to become like children, surely, in part, these are the qualities he wants to find in us.

Let us look at them in more detail under three headings: openness, immediacy and freedom of spirit.

Openness

Openness to the world around

To walk with a child is to see the world through renewed eyes. Sights, sounds, big events (like the movement of smoke across the sky), and small activities (like a raindrop running down a window), which we usually pass without a second glance, take on a new life. To be small enough is to find wonder in everything, and because so much is new and unknown and not understood, a sense of awe is a natural response. These words of Korczak are a moving example:

He is inexperienced.
He drops a glass on the floor.
Then something extraordinary happens.
The glass has disappeared and
    completely different objects have appeared in its place!
He leans over, picks up a piece of glass,
    cuts his finger which begins to bleed.
Everything is full of mysteries and surprises.[10]

If we broke a glass and then cut our finger, we would be upset or annoyed, scurrying to clear up the broken glass and hunt for a plaster. A child, on the other hand, discovers surprises in the broken glass, the cut finger and the blood. What a gift to be able to experience the world with such an open heart! Recently, I totally lost the attention of a group of children I was working with when one of them managed to swat a fly in the air. The whole group gathered around to see the spectacle of the stunned fly lying on its back, feebly waving its legs.

It is also important to realize that such openness, and the

emergence of wonder and awe in a child, are not limited to nature and the natural world, and are certainly not limited to objects of beauty. As Korczak observed, 'Everything is interesting to him.' Things that we would consider gross or ugly, aspects of inner-city life that we would never expect to elicit a sense of wonder—among such objects and in such places children find things to inspire fascination and wonder. Imagine, then, how much more amazing and awe-inspiring it is to see an ocean, acres of green field, a night sky, or a waterfall for the first time. Our inner-city children need to be offered the privilege of this dimension of wonder, too. I recall the expressions of an adult friend of mine as we drove east out of London through the seemingly endless estates of Dagenham and Becontree—blocks and blocks of flats, but common land around them with cows grazing. 'Cor, isn't it lovely to be out in the country? Look at the cows!' Not what I would have called country by any stretch of the imagination, but it was, relative to my friend's home surroundings. Visits to real countryside, to the seaside, to hills and mountains, need to be part of our urban kids' experiences of growing up—maybe for a day, maybe for a week at a summer camp.

Openness to feelings

It is really children who are the princes of feelings, the poets and thinkers.[11]

Children tend to be very open with their feelings, rather than censoring expression of them as we adults tend to do. They will freely express their emotions—crying, laughing, sulking, giggling and so on—as and when they feel them. They also exhibit an honesty and directness that puts us to shame (as we can be very two-faced and insincere) and embarrasses us—as, for example, when a child makes (in adult terms) an untimely and inappropriate comment. Bel Mooney, author of the series of books about eight-year-old Kitty, captures this perfectly.

'Kitty! You're the naughtiest child in England!' said Mum.

'How do you know? You haven't met them all,' said Kitty.

'Oh, very clever,' said Mum, in her irritated voice.

'Thanks, Mum!' said Kitty.

Her mother opened her mouth—then closed it again. Kitty thought she looked like a fish, and said so. It made her laugh. Then Mum got up from the table, and started to come towards her—so Kitty thought it was time to leave the room…

The trouble with people (she thought) is that they never understand jokes. She wasn't trying to be nasty, or cheeky, or clever. She was only trying to be funny, and that was different.[12]

Children also have a keen intuition and are very perceptive. This may be because their ability to pick up non-verbal cues leads them to 'hear' beyond words (as we shall see later in exploring non-verbal messages). A child will sense when our patience is about to evaporate, or when their pushing a little further will actually get us to give in, to laugh, to concede a point. Again Korczak:

A child knows his environment; its moods, habits and failings.
He knows it and, one should add, he exploits it skilfully.
He can intuit kindness, detect deceit and has a sense of the ridiculous.
He is able to read a face,
*   in the same way a farmer reads the sky to forecast the weather.*
This is because he too has been observing and investigating us for many years.[13]

Children's perceptivity can also mean that they will be aware when we are not feeling well or are worried about something. Within a family, it can happen almost at an unconscious level as the child senses that something is amiss and that the atmosphere of the home has changed as a result. This can lead to troubled or disruptive behaviour, as the child feels unsafe but does not have the awareness or language to identify what is disturbing him. Later on, we will look further at how the child handles feelings.

Openness to people

Children's natural response is to be open, friendly and welcoming to other people (unless they have learned or been taught otherwise). It is an immense privilege, as an adult, to be welcomed and accepted by a child. I recall the time I walked into McDonald's to hear cries of 'Kathryn!' from the food counter as two little girls detached themselves from their father and came running over to fling their arms around me. I felt ten feet tall! Alongside being open to people comes trust and, again, unless they have learned otherwise, children are naturally trusting. Meeting children for the first time and being taken by the hand and invited to join in a game is an unspoken example of trust. Children sense who can be trusted and who is worthy of their invitation to 'come and play'.

Immediacy

Immediacy in the here and now

Nouwen's observations of the children he met in Peru, quoted at the beginning of this section, highlight three important points. Children challenge us to live in the present. As adults, we often live everywhere but in the present: we live in yesterday; we live in tomorrow; we live parallel with ourselves in what someone else is doing, or in what else we could be doing. In the process, we miss the gift of the moment. The reason time seems to pass more and more quickly the older we get is that we are always looking somewhere other than the 'now'. Time lasts for ever to children because they are totally absorbed in the current moment.

Nouwen also commented on the children's ability to be fully present to him. Children present themselves to us with 100 per cent of their being, or not at all. They don't pretend to be 'present' if they don't want to be and they are not interested. How often have you been with another adult and sensed that they were not fully present? They may appear to be, but you are aware of their eyes darting off here and there; they make the right noises, but their heart is not in the conversation.

Finally, Nouwen's children invited him to 'celebrate life where it is found'. We can all celebrate life, but often we go looking for it in order to celebrate it. Children don't have to look for it. It is there, all around them, waiting to be enjoyed and celebrated. Their gift is that they can see it. 'Look at the birds in the sky… Look how the wild flowers grow,' said Jesus. 'Don't worry about tomorrow'—or yesterday, we might add (Matthew 6:26, 28, 34). Celebrate life here and now, where it is found. Nouwen had the wisdom to identify that in this ability to live life in the present lies the great healing power that children have. He went to Peru worried that he might be overwhelmed and depressed by the poverty he would encounter, unsure how he would cope with the misery.

But God showed me something else first: affectionate, open and playful children who are telling me about love and life in ways no book was ever able to do. I now realize that only when I enter with the children into their joy will I be able to enter also with them into their poverty and pain. God obviously wants me to walk into the world of suffering with a little child on each hand.[14]

Korczak echoes the same theme:

If your own life is like a graveyard to you—
Leave children free to see it as a pasture.[15]

Immediacy in spontaneity

Closely related to 'the here and now' is spontaneity—the gift children have for taking the ordinary and making it extraordinary on the spur of the moment. It may be a cardboard box that becomes a castle, a pattern of words that becomes a chant, a single word that becomes a game, a few simple notes that become an aria, a falling leaf that becomes an aeroplane, an accidental knock that becomes a wrestling match, a look that becomes an argument. The key to spontaneity is that it is unpremeditated. We listen to a child and think, 'Wow! Where did that come from?' The creative nature of the child is closely linked with this spontaneity (see below).

Immediacy in simplicity

As adults, we are very good at analysing and dissecting issues. We need a lot of explanations before we will accept information. Children will accept things at face value—they will accept information as given. They do not need (and often do not want) a lot of extra 'adult' information. Even now, my daughter (nearly 20) will sometimes preface a question to me with, 'I just want the answer, Mum.' She has had too many years of an over-enthusiastic mother wanting to use every opportunity to cram in a little more information. I have a suspicion that we often overload our Sunday sessions with children by following our adult need for analysis and explanations. We seem to forget that 'God in his wisdom made it impossible for people to know him by means of their own wisdom', and that 'God purposely chose what the world considers nonsense in order to shame the wise' (1 Corinthians 1:21, 27, GNB).

We also seem to forget that children can find a relationship with God easy and uncomplicated. Jerome Berryman highlights this issue in his book, *Godly Play*. Speaking of two boys engaging with the parable of the mustard seed, he observes:

We adults talk 'about' such things more conceptually and with greater differentiation and abstraction than children can. It may be that these adult abilities are not an improvement but a disability when it comes to coping with existential issues. The ability to talk about existential issues turns personal experiences into abstractions.[16]

Understanding the difference between talking about existential issues and experiencing them is crucial when working with children. We need to be able to leave children free to do the experiencing.

Perhaps one of our adult difficulties is the worry that children may come up with the 'wrong' answer. We may be accustomed to believing that children need be told the 'purpose' of a parable or the 'meaning' of a story—that it is not safe to leave children to discover it for themselves. Yet is this not precisely what Jesus did time and again, as he told parables and stories to the crowds and challenged them to see, hear and understand for themselves? A child may discover an insight that we as adults may not see, and we need to allow space for this to happen. We must remember that 'the child's encounter with God is a relationship that is beyond the team's control'.[17]

Freedom of spirit

Freedom of spirit in creativity

In the boundless creativity of children we see one of the qualities that most clearly illustrates their spiritual dimension, because God is, above all, creative. If the ultimate in creativity is creating something out of nothing (Genesis 1:1), you will have seen it in any situation where you have tried to remove all distractions in order to encourage a child to concentrate! Children can create an activity out of a piece of fluff or a dead fly. It almost seems as if there can be no such thing as an empty room for children. They will find something to occupy them, something with which to create. A child's creativity finds its greatest expression in play. In fact, play is 're-creation'. Berryman speaks of play as being 'at the edge of knowing and being, where mystery begins and limit can end'.[18] Play is the way a child learns. Essentially, this means that as children re-create, so they learn to understand and interact with the world around them.

Freedom of spirit in imagination

Imagination, the entry point to creativity, is one of the greatest gifts within our spirituality, and we see it in its fullness in children. The ability to use images to move from the here and now to another place and time, to become something or someone else, means that the entire world and beyond is ours in our mind and in our mind's eye. We can be and do the impossible with imagination—and we can do it anywhere. Imagination can be a lifeline to children who are starved of nourishing relationships or experiences, because through it they can enter into other worlds. It can provide security in a world of constant change. By the time I was 17, I had lived in eight different places in three different countries, and I had changed schools five times. Escaping into the imaginary world of books became my way of finding security and stability, because I could take my imaginary worlds with me into each new situation. Imagination is, above all, a means whereby children can allow their creativity to have full rein.

Freedom of spirit in integration

We have already noted that children don't make our adult distinctions between what is secular and what is sacred, between the 'everyday' and the 'set apart'. They approach life as an integrated whole. As a result, they are themselves integrated, and with this comes the reality that 'what you see is what you get'. Until they learn otherwise, children don't see the need to become something they are not in order simply to please an adult. Their inner and outer worlds are one. We can know where we stand with children—what they like and don't like, what interests them and what doesn't. Children challenge us to be truly integrated, to live honest lives, such that we don't become someone else simply to impress or for gain.

Freedom of spirit in love

Finally, children have an infinite capacity for love, because God, in whose image they are created, is love. Their love is given freely and without reserve. It is not conditional and temperamental. And as the child loves, so he or she needs to be loved in return and offered all the nourishment that accompanies true loving, so that s/he can enter the fullness of life that God intends.

And what else can the essence of the soul be, if not the whole universe, but without bounds. This is the contradictory nature of human beings, who have arisen from dust, but in whom God has set up residence.[19]

A researched approach to spirituality

Through the Children's Spirituality Project, David Hay and Rebecca Nye set about identifying what constitutes children's spirituality within a secular culture. They identified a number of interrelated themes or categories of spiritual sensitivity, which they used as a starting point in their interviews with children, believing them to be key elements in anyone's spiritual life: awareness-sensing, mystery-sensing and value-sensing. It is interesting that the core content of these themes is broadly similar to the themes identified above (openness, immediacy and freedom of spirit), which arose from my hands-on work with children.[20] This would seem to suggest that the themes emerging from both approaches do accurately represent what we call children's spirituality.

So, to recap, we have before us the child created in the image of God, a deeply spiritual being, gifted by God with qualities of openness, awareness, sensitivity, joy, trust, imagination and honesty. However, children are not consciously aware that these are unique qualities with which they have been gifted. They are simply living life day by day as it comes to them, in the ways they know best. Perhaps an awareness that they experience the world differently begins to dawn when they discover how difficult it is for adults to enter their world. Then, as they grow older and experience more of the adult world, they discover that the qualities valued by adults are different. New and different learning has to take place if they are to survive.

Let us now take a step sideways and think about the developing child.

PART TWO

The developing child

The child has a primary need from the very beginning of her life to be regarded and respected as the person she really is at any given time.
ALICE MILLER[21]

What is a child? What is our perspective on the child? Maybe we've never consciously given much thought to these questions. A child is obviously an immature human being, needing to be nurtured, protected and educated until he or she becomes a mature, adult human being. While this is true as a broad biological framework, it is only part of the story. Children have been seen differently at different periods in history and in different parts of the world. They have been seen as of low status and as vulnerable, unwanted babies to be exposed or killed. Gender has made a difference: girl babies may be valued more or less highly than boys. Their value may lie in their coming of age: they may be valued chiefly for the economic contribution that they make to society. They may be valued as an insurance against the parents' old age. They may be valued for their potential to make a good marriage. They may be valued for the status they bring to the family, for their looks, their intelligence, or their health. They may be valued if they can be seen but not heard![22]

Traditionally, children have been valued for what they would become—their instrumental worth. In agricultural societies, children are expected to play their part in caring for younger siblings and in helping as part of the family workforce, increasingly taking on adult responsibilities. As societies became industrialized, children played—and, in some parts of the world, still are playing—an important role in the factories, keeping the machines running. Even today, for all our insight into child psychology and child development, our free market capitalism in the West values children in terms of their contribution to society. As Dawn DeVries points out, 'Children are primarily seen as products, consumers or burdens'.[23] She points to the increasing potential for parents to order 'designer babies' as products—the child who is highly intelligent, beautiful, with the right combination of genes to repay the parents for the time, effort and risk they put into raising the child. We have only to look at marketing trends and watch television adverts to see that children as consumers are key players in increasing sales and profit margins for large companies. De Vries points to the infant and the child in poverty as burdens: non-producers and a drain on the economy.

Then there are those who see the child as having intrinsic worth. Regardless of what children become, they have value in the here and now, simply for who they are. Clearly, all of Jesus' words and actions in relation to children indicate that he saw in children their intrinsic value. This is surely the heart of the gospel—that we see each child as having infinite worth simply for who he or she is.

But how does this work out in practice? How do we really see children? Do we place more value on the child who is accommodating and easy to manage, because we know that the end product will be that we get through our group session with a minimum of aggravation and disruption? Are we in danger of thinking that kids who are a hassle or who don't contribute anything (in our terms) are a burden? Are we in danger of using a product or programme that simply entertains kids without going any deeper?

Valuing children for their intrinsic worth is not as easy as it sounds. We are brought up in a culture that values outcomes: if you can measure it, then it has value. We can see this in our education system: league tables, SATs and exams. Looking at and valuing children simply for who they are is rarely done.

Think of a child in your group, perhaps one on the fringes for whatever reason, perhaps one whom you have not fully 'seen'. Now take a sheet of paper and make a list of all the qualities in that child that speak of his or her intrinsic worth. If it helps, look at the child through God's eyes, not in the sense of seeing what s/he can become, but seeing who s/he is now. Each of your children needs someone who will look at them like this.

A hundred children—a hundred people
Who are not 'maybe sometime',
Not 'not now', not 'tomorrow',
But are here and now, today
People who already exist.[24]

The hungers children have

How do we begin to understand and value children for who they really are? One way is to discover what they need to receive from us. Eric Berne, the creator of Transactional Analysis, identifies a number of 'hungers' with which a child comes into the world. These hungers are psychological needs that must be fulfilled if the child is to develop into a healthy, whole individual, but they also have a physiological basis that makes them necessary for survival. Berne identified six hungers: recognition, contact, stimulus, structure, incident and sexual hunger. Subsequent Transactional Analysis therapists have included creativity and spirituality as separate hungers, although Berne seems to imply that they are part of the other six.[25]

Recognition hunger

Each child comes into the world with a need for an acknowledgment of his or her existence. She or he needs to be recognized for who s/he is—a unique individual. All children need a significant other person (adult or peer) to see in them something that makes them stand out in the world, someone who values them for being who they are as individuals, rather than being just one of many or, worse still, someone else.

This need can start to be met even before birth, as the mother comes to know and talk with the baby in her womb, but it is met in earnest from the moment of birth as the newborn baby begins to bond with the mother. 'Within a minute of birth babies can identify their mother and are more comforted by her than by a stranger. Within two minutes they are straining their neck to study her face.'[26] Alice Miller, the child therapist who has written extensively on child-rearing and abuse, says, 'Every child has a legitimate need to be noticed, understood, taken seriously and respected by his mother.' She borrows from Donald Winnicott the image of 'mirroring', where the child gazes into the mother's face and finds himself there. 'If a child is lucky enough to grow up with a mirroring, available mother who is at the child's disposal [as part of his development] ... then a healthy self-feeling can gradually develop in the growing child.'[27]

Recognizing and valuing the child in this way at such an early age is laying crucial foundations for the development of a sense of self-worth in the child. A sense that who I am matters, that I have significance in the world and that other people notice me is fundamental to basic survival and healthy development. Different individuals need different levels of recognition. We hear about the baby who cries constantly until he is picked up, contrasted unfavourably with the placid, contented baby who never cries. When my son was just two or three years old, I recall the amazement of colleagues as he would sit beside me through meetings, contentedly munching apples and looking at books, satisfied with occasional chats and nods. My daughter, however, was well known among the other parents as I collected my son from school: she could be heard coming long before she was seen. One is not 'better' than the other. They simply have different levels of need for recognition. Unfortunately, we don't always realize this, so our praise is reserved for the child who is easier to handle, while the more demanding child is told off.

These patterns carry on into later life. We may see that a child who thrives on a high level of recognition, of 'being noticed', may be the centre of attention among a group of friends in the pub, or may take on a job that involves being in the public eye. A child requiring a lower level of recognition might be quite content with a low-profile career that does not necessarily involve being noticed.

The opposite of recognition is indifference, which is devastating for a child. Because the hunger for recognition is so powerful, a child will go to any lengths to secure it. It is part of every child's birthright, and if children cannot obtain it legitimately, they will force the world to give it to them. Some of the children we find most difficult and disruptive in our groups could well be children who have experienced little quality recognition at home, or whose home life has been so dysfunctional that no one has had the awareness, time or energy to give them recognition. Consequently, in order to avoid indifference, they have resorted to negative behaviours in a search for notice. Negative recognition is better than no recognition at all. Having been starved of quality attention and valuing for so long, they simply do not know (and maybe have never known) what it is to be simply valued for who they are. They have only ever learnt to seek negative recognition.

The most significant result, when a child's hunger for recognition is met, is that it helps to build a sense of self-worth or self-esteem. For some reason, Christians have a lot of hang-ups about self-esteem, especially those brought up in the classic evangelical mould, where they have been taught that they have no value outside of Christ. Valuing oneself and building self-worth is often perceived to be putting human beings at the centre and above God—yet we are made in God's image, just a little lower than God himself, says Psalm 8. And what do the following passages reveal if not the wonderful truth that God recognizes, sees and knows us from the very beginning of our lives—and even before?

When my bones were being formed,
Carefully put together in my mother's womb,
When I was growing there in secret,

You knew that I was there—
You saw me before I was born.
PSALM 139:15–16 (GNB)

I chose you before I gave you life, and before you were born I selected you.
JEREMIAH 1:5 (GNB)

Surely this is ample evidence that God's care and love for us, even before birth, warrants our having a sense of our own value, knowing that we are loved, created and sustained by God.

One definition of self-esteem is 'one's assessment of the extent to which one is lovable and capable. Self-esteem is nourished by recognizing one's own lovableness and capabilities and by being recognized as lovable and capable by other people.'[28] Too many children have never been recognized as lovable and capable by others, never mind being taught how to recognize these qualities in themselves. Instead, they receive a steady diet of negative messages, which tell them that they are worthless or that they simply shouldn't be: 'Not you again!'; 'Get lost!'; 'What are you doing here?' We will look in more detail, in the next section, at the messages children receive.

Contact hunger

Closely related to recognition hunger is the hunger for contact or touch. The physiological basis for this is that when we touch another person, skin to skin, there is an exchange of infra-red rays that is both pleasurable and energizing. Contact is essential to both our physical and our emotional health. The baby growing in the womb for nine months has experienced a close and nourishing contact with the mother, both physically and psychologically. When he or she is born, this needs to continue. Babies need to be held, cuddled, touched and handled. Research shows that the skin is the baby's 'first medium of communication with the outside world'.[29] A recent article in *The Times* newspaper refers to 'kangaroo care', a technique used to help newborn babies to sleep more soundly and develop more healthily. Referring to the care a mother kangaroo gives to her joey, mothers (and fathers) are encouraged to lay the baby naked between their breasts to ensure maximum skin contact. Research at the University of Haifa in Israel showed that babies cuddled in this way sleep better and are more relaxed, and their motor system develops better in the days after birth.[30]

Babies who do not receive adequate touching are more susceptible to a condition known as 'marasmus', or wasting away due to a protein-energy deficiency. This leads to depression, appetite and weight loss, and eventually death. In meeting the baby's hunger for contact through touching, cuddling and holding, the mother is effectively saying, 'You matter. You are important. I will care for you.' This is what every child needs to experience from birth. Like positive recognition, it builds the foundations for a sense of self-worth and helps the child experience that everything that goes to make up 'me' is OK.

Touch is by no means always life-giving, however. Many children experience little, if any, positive touch. As babies they may be roughly handled by a fraught, over-stressed carer, or they may be left to cry, with no contact, by a parent who is unable to cope or who believes (mistakenly) that to do so avoids 'spoiling' the child. Consequently, the basic sense of safety and security needed for healthy development at a very early age is missing: the child experiences that no one is there to meet his or her needs.

Such children may be more used to a clip round the ear or a slap than a hug. They may have experienced physical or sexual abuse involving inappropriate or intrusive touching, so that their experience of touch is linked with a confusing combination of feelings of shame, pleasure, guilt, fear and vulnerability. Because the hunger for contact is so strong, however, in some situations negative touching may be preferable to no touch at all. As a result, these children may only know how to touch others with physical force or with violence, or with developmentally inappropriate sexual behaviour. The sense of their own value and identity, their boundaries and their ability to relate to others may be fundamentally damaged.

The issue of touch can be problematic to those working with children. We may see children who principally experience negative touch, and we long to offer them the loving touch in the Old Testament picture of God's love for his children: 'I drew them to me with affection and love. I picked them up and held them to my cheek; I bent down to them and fed them' (Hosea 11:4, GNB). We look at Jesus' ministry in the Gospels and see the many situations in which he touched those who were suffering, who needed help or affirmation—the crippled woman (Luke 13:10–14), the children (Luke 18:15–17), Simon's mother-in-law (Mark 1:29–31), the man with the skin disease (Matthew 8:1–4), Jairus' daughter and the two blind men (Matthew 9:18–31). Jesus certainly recognized the importance of touch as a healing action, and did not hold back in using it. Yet we are often constrained, by the requirements of the Children Act, from giving the loving, affirming touch that many of our children need. We feel frustrated, knowing that there may be no other context in which some children can experience healthy touch.

One way in which we can give such children the experience of positive touch is through the use of puppets, in which they can be free to express themselves and to respond to the puppets using touch. Modelling positive and respectful touch between parents and group leaders may also practically demonstrate a way of relating that some children may never otherwise see or experience. For those working with very young children, it is natural ro respond with a cuddle if a child is hurt, holding hands, an arm around the shoulders, provided such touch is given in an appropriate, safe context when others are around.

Stimulus hunger

Stimulus hunger relates to our biological need for stimulation through our five senses. We were created with a need to see, hear, taste, smell and touch the world around us. Stimulation of the brain is essential not only for healthy development but also for our very survival. Perhaps that is why the very first biblical picture of man and woman is set in the garden of Eden, where the surrounding world must have offered endless opportunities for the senses to be nourished. Where there is insufficient stimulation, the brain gradually shuts down the senses: if they are not used, they begin to atrophy. You may recall the tragic photographs of infants in their cots in the Romanian orphanages following the overthrow of President Ceausescu. Lacking any stimulation in the way of touch, activity and meaningful human interaction, they survived physically but had lost the ability to relate to the outside world. As a result, they did not know how to relate, respond or play. They presented a blank face to the world or found what stimulation they could through head-banging or other repetitive actions.

We learn about and enjoy the world around us through our senses. Children use their senses to the full: there is just so much to see, hear, taste, touch and smell that is new.

Because a child cannot be idle, he will poke into every corner,
Inspect every nook and cranny,
Find things and ask questions about them.
Everything seems interesting to him.[31]

Part of helping children to live a rich life is to offer them as wide a variety of appropriate new experiences as possible, while they are still open to them. As we get older, we use some of our senses less, or perhaps in more limited contexts. Take the sense of smell, for example. Children will get into a new car and vigorously sniff the smell of newness. They will go up to someone, sniff them and comment on how nice (or otherwise!) they smell. When I was a child in Japan, my friends all commented on the fact that I smelt like butter. As adults, our sense of smell may often become a lot less acute: we may use it less and be a lot more inhibited in acknowledging how it affects us.

We are also far more restrained in what, who and how we touch. We already know what wet paint feels like, so we don't touch it. We know that a candle flame is hot, so we don't touch it. We know that wet mud feels squelchy and slimy, so we don't touch it. But in not touching, we also shut ourselves off from experiences that can newly stimulate us. Squelchy mud may feel very different when you're an adult from the way it did when you were a child.

We do, however, need to find a balance: over-stimulation can be as harmful as under-stimulation. Many aspects of contemporary culture can batter a child's senses. A steady diet of loud music, flashing lights, constant movement on a screen, conversations held at fever pitch, several storylines running concurrently in a soap, the buzz of chatter online—such activity can lead to a sense of monotony, emptiness or boredom when it stops. So we find children who don't know how to stop, to appreciate space and silence, to be still, simply to be. The diagnosis of ADD or ADHD (Attention Deficit Disorder or Attention Deficit Hyperactivity Disorder) in children seems to be on the increase. Certainly this is a recognized condition which needs to be treated medically. However, we may well wonder whether the condition of children at the milder end of the spectrum can be attributed to over-stimulation. We all know of children who, when they come into our group, seem to bring an aura of hyperactivity, over-excitement and high energy with them, which is very contagious. They may well be demonstrating the reality that their lives are chaotic and over-stimulated, and what is needed are structures and boundaries to help them contain themselves.

Structure hunger

Just as children need sensory stimulation and all its accompanying richness, nourishment and excitement, so they need structure in their lives to help them manage the stimulation and live their lives in a meaningful way. Structure hunger is all about how we manage our time and how we achieve a sense of security and certainty in our lives. When this hunger is adequately met, we feel safe about the experiences that each day brings us and the people we meet, because we have set in place the structures that enable us to cope in these encounters.

Eric Berne identified six different types of behaviour that make up our way of giving structure to our lives. They are based on our relationships with others and may be seen as points on a spectrum, from least meaningful contact to greatest contact.

- The first is *withdrawal*, and refers to times when we choose to be on our own physically, or when we might just drift off into our own world in our thoughts or daydreams.
- The second is *rituals*, where we engage with others but at a formal, ritualized level, with stock phrases—rather like the checkout person in the supermarket who says, 'Have a nice day'.
- The third is *pastimes*. These also are quite ritualistic but involve a little more warmth and engagement. They may include the types of conversation that a parent has with other parents at the school gate, where we chat about a child's sleeping patterns, or where children talk about the local football team's recent match. These are important behaviours, as they can signal the beginning of a greater intimacy.
- *Activities* are the next level of time structuring, where we engage together with others in a common activity, perhaps going swimming or playing football together.
- The fifth type of time structuring is when people engage in what Berne called '*games*'. This term is perhaps more usefully explained as 'psychological games', and is about the negative, repetitive patterns we get into in our relationships with others, where the outcome is predictable and familiar. At a very simple level, an example would be the child who, on coming into our group, automatically punches a younger child (who immediately bursts into tears). At an outcome level, the older child responds, 'I'm always getting told off', and the younger child responds, 'I always get picked on'. Thus their views of themselves are

reinforced: one is always criticized; one is always victim. This is the 'game' they play. This happens to all of us, and we need to learn to be aware of when we are being drawn into a game, so that we can make a choice not to join in.

- The greatest level of contact comes with *intimacy*, which involves a close relationship of openness, trust and lack of defence between two individuals.

As is the case with all hungers, different personalities need different combinations of these ways of structuring time. Some individuals need more time and space to be on their own, to withdraw into their own world and disengage from the world around them. Others are more gregarious and enjoy engaging in activities with others, joining clubs, being in a busy classroom. Still others need one or two close, intimate relationships. A healthy individual is one who includes space for meeting each need in the way time is structured. A balance is needed. Being aware of the time-structuring behaviour of the different children in our group helps us to plan a programme that both meets the children's personal preferences and gives them a healthy balance. We need to be aware, for example, that the child who withdraws or daydreams perhaps comes from an overcrowded home where there is no space just to be with his or her own thoughts. The child who wants all your attention just for herself perhaps also comes from a busy household with younger siblings, and never experiences an adult with time just to listen and be a friend. Clearly, there may also be other explanations for such behaviour, but we need to be aware of the effect of structure hunger.

Incident hunger

As children of missionary parents, we used to spend our summers up in the mountains where the air was cooler. Those few weeks were the highlight of my year. When they were over and I had to go back to school, my stock moan was, 'Now I've nothing to look forward to!' I now realize that my incident hunger was not adequately fulfilled.

Incident hunger is related to, but different from, stimulus hunger. Whereas stimulus hunger involves nourishment of our senses, incident hunger looks for something that is new, unexpected and somewhat destabilizing. Our need for structure provides security and certainty, but the downside can be monotony and repetitiveness. Our hunger for incident meets our need for adventure. As with all hungers, different individuals have different levels of need for incident. A summer holiday in the mountains might have been enough incident for some people but, as a child, I needed something ongoing through the year to fill my need. A walk along a beach might be enough for one person, whereas another might prefer to do a bungee jump.

How often have we heard children say, 'I'm bored!' Our heart sinks as we think about the time we spent carefully preparing activities, but they may well be expressing a need for incident to relieve the 'everyday-ness' of activities, rather than reflecting on the quality of our ideas. If children cannot get this need met in positive ways, they may create their own incident to relieve the boredom! I recall the child who 'escaped' from our after-school club with a younger child in tow, shut the little boy in the lift of the nearby tower block and sent him up to the 15th floor, calling forth screams of fear. That was adequate incident for both of them! Many of our children grow up lacking experiences of positive incident—that is, new and exciting adventures. Parents may not have the time, energy or initiative to plan for or suggest such an activity to their child. As a result, the kids will create their own incident, large or small, which might well be—though not intentionally—destructive.

Sexual hunger

Finally, each of us is created by God with a sexual hunger, the need for sexual contact with others and the meeting of our sexual needs.

This is an area frequently avoided by Christians, to the detriment of our work with children. The fact that the United Kingdom has the highest rate of teenage pregnancies in Europe may be explained in part by ignorance on the part of teenagers.

The following letter appeared in *The Guardian* (27 March 1998), giving an example of the type of letters received by teen magazines such as *Sugar* and *Bliss*.

I'm only 14 years old and I have this problem about sex. If you sleep with a guy and don't have sex, can you get pregnant? And when you kiss a guy, I mean not just a kiss, but kissing with a guy for quite a long time, can you get pregnant too? All my friends say if you have sex with a guy, you stand a chance of getting pregnant. Is this true?

Why such ignorance? Avoidance on our part does not make the issue go away.

Three words we need to bear in mind when addressing sexual hunger are awareness, integration and normality. We need to be aware that children's sexuality is part and parcel of who they are as human beings. Feeding at the mother's breast, discovering how little girls are different to little boys, finding out that riding a rocking horse can give a good feeling 'down there'—all of these are about sexual discovery for a young child. As parents particularly, we need to normalize reference to such experiences and our discussion of them. If the message children receive is that Mum and Dad don't feel safe talking about sex, that they always change the subject or 'I get told off for asking questions', then they will shut down and/or go elsewhere for information. If, on the other hand, children are exposed to sexual innuendo and the sexual activities of their parents in inappropriate ways, then their response to issues around sexuality may be inappropriate to their developmental stage.

As we have learned, children are highly sensual individuals, exploring their world by means of their senses. They need to grow up with an experience of safe, nurturing touch. Little girls need to be able to romp with Dad in a safe, non-sexual way. Little boys need lots of warm, intimate hugs from Mum. Then, as they grow into adolescence, they will be able to separate out their need for nurturing touch from their need for sexual touch and find both appropriately.

Children today are bombarded with messages that relate to sex and their sexuality. It is well known that teen magazines, such as those referred to above, are read by children as young as nine and ten. They tell you everything from what clothes and make-up you should be wearing to how to have safe sex. Children who have no other source of information look to such magazines for guidance on sexuality. Song lyrics refer to sex and sexuality as naturally as they might to walking down the street. Television soaps are full of affairs, characters dropping in and out of relationships and, often, in and out of bed. It would seem that an awareness of the power of sexual hunger is normative in the world to which many of our children are exposed, but it is certainly not normative in the world of many Christians.

It is essential that we work harder at integrating an understanding of this hunger into our own lives and set it firmly within the context of a Christian value system, so that we can counter the many un-helpful and unhealthy messages a child receives with alternatives that are positive and nurturing. Children need to feel free to talk about issues relating to their sexuality, and we need to be able to respond in a natural, normal manner. This is often very difficult for us: the baggage we carry makes it a loaded subject, whereas we can talk quite easily about similarly important issues around honesty or friendship. We need to set boundaries for our children and help children to set their own. In spite of the backlash we might get when we set a boundary, deep down our ten- or eleven-year-old will be relieved to be able to say, 'I'm not allowed to come to a mixed party at your house when your parents aren't there', or, 'I'm not allowed to watch an 18 DVD.' We need to give children ideas about what to say in tricky situations. Our words will remain with and support the child.

Unfortunately, many of the children we work with will have grown up in situations that are anything but nurturing in terms of their sexuality. We will be working with children who are overly sexually aware, do not know how to distinguish between sexual touch and nurturing touch, or perhaps have only known sex as something to be giggled at or as the subject of dirty jokes. As appropriate, such children need to be helped to see a different way of understanding sex. To help them in this way, we need to be aware and integrated ourselves, so that we can talk openly and normally about such matters.

The life patterns children develop

- Kyle is six. He hurtles into the group to play with Spiderman. Tom decides to join in. Kyle elbows him out of the way. 'Geroff!' Tom retreats to a distance, then tries again. This time Kyle lunges at him with his shoulder and a few choice expletives.

- Shanice is eight. She comes into the group and sits by herself at a table. She starts an activity but keeps her head down. She avoids eye contact. She only speaks when spoken to, and her voice is so soft that you can hardly hear her.

- Cassie is five. She dissolves into tears and goes into a sulk every time she doesn't get her way. She's only happy when she has 100 per cent of your attention. She has a cunning way of annoying other children when she thinks you aren't looking, and blatantly denying it when challenged.

- Ben is nearly eleven but small for his age. On a good day, he is a delight. On a bad day, he spreads chaos throughout the club. He will saunter through the room, grabbing a child's activity and running off with it. He will disrupt the football game. He will flood the loos. Ben roams the city streets alone at ten and eleven o'clock at night.

I am filled with unbounded gratitude to this girl.
There is nothing special about her, nothing to attract attention.
An ordinary face, average mind, little imagination, absolute lack of
Tenderness.
Nothing that makes children adorable.
But it is nature, its eternal laws,
God, speaking through this unspectacular child,
Just as through any scrubby bush growing by the roadside.
Thank you, for being just as you are, just ordinary. [32]

Kyle, Shanice, Cassie and Ben are just ordinary children—similar, no doubt, to those with whom you work. Sometimes it is difficult to discern and hold on to their spirituality. Where does it vanish to?

As children grow, they develop a life script. This means that, based on their experiences and the way they perceive those experiences, they make decisions about how life will be in the future. The term 'script' comes from Transactional Analysis literature and refers to the way in which a child will come to see the world. Once children have become more independent of their care-givers and peers, more self-aware and in a position to make their own choices, they may exercise their autonomy and choose to live their own life rather than follow the script. In the meantime, the use of the term 'script' indicates that children are playing a role determined for them by their experiences and circumstances. 'The script is a personal life plan, developed mainly before the age of seven under parental, familial, social, cultural and religious pressure... The script is "written" in early childhood, rehearsed and revised in later childhood and performed in adulthood.' [33]

So children have experiences and receive messages from the people in their world. The way they perceive and experience those messages will determine the way in which their script will be formed. If they have learned by the age of seven that adults are not consistent or trustworthy, then they may have difficulty in forming positive relationships with adults. As adults themselves, they may then have problems with authority figures. If they have received a message that they are not expected to be as clever as an older sibling, this may very well become a self-fulfilling prophecy.

Pause for a minute to absorb the significance of this fact: a child's life script—their way of seeing the world—is principally developed before the age of seven. A young child is dependent and vulnerable, lacking in experience of the world, totally reliant on his or her care-givers, yet the foundations for the whole of future life are laid by the age of seven. This must impact the use of our time and resources with under-sevens, and it must also challenge us to consider how we support the parents and other care-givers in this most important of all tasks, bringing up children.

These findings are reinforced by research into the way in which the brain develops. We know that when a baby is born, there is still a considerable amount of 'wiring up' to be completed. The synaptic connections, or links, between the cells in the brain are not finally completed until the young person is in their late teens. A child's experiences help to complete these connections, and are affected by factors such as environment, temperament and age. Negative, abusive or traumatic experiences will mean that some connections are lost or organized differently in order for the child to cope. 'The child's brain is most plastic in the early years… to allow for maximum adaptability to experience. At eight months, the brain has more synaptic connections… than at any other time of life as the child prepares to meet any and all new situations with maximum cognitive flexibility.'[34] If the environment is not stimulating or care-givers are not nurturing, then synaptic connections may be lost. When trauma or abuse occurs at periods critical for development—for example, before the age of three when bonding with care-givers needs to take place—the effect will be longer lasting and more profound.

Think again of the condition of the Romanian infants in the orphanages referred to above, where they had become non-responsive or had resorted to head-banging as a response to the total lack of stimulation in their environment. Research shows also that experiences from the pre-verbal earliest days, weeks and months of a baby's life—even experiences and sounds before birth—enter a place of 'body memory' within the child. They are held unconsciously within the child, but their effect may appear at some point in later life, seemingly from nowhere. These memories could be about a core sense of safety, or a core sense of fear and loss, depending on the nature of the child's experiences.

The messages children receive

Returning to Kyle, Shanice, Cassie and Ben, let us explore some of the types of messages they will have received as they have grown up.

Verbal and non-verbal messages

Children will hear us saying one thing, but the non-verbal message may well say something else. 'Mum, you there?' calls the child. 'Yes,' replies the mother, but that 'yes' can give many different messages, depending on the tone of voice and the gestures that accompany it. It can mean, 'Yes, I'm here and available to you', but it can also mean, 'Not you again', 'Don't bother me!', 'I'm tired out' or 'I'm fed up with you.' It can even mean 'Shut up!' A baby in arms may hear, 'Aren't you sweet? I'll look after you', but the non-verbal message communicated by the way the baby is held may say, 'I can't cope with your crying any longer' or 'You're not safe here.' Korczak expresses this dual message perfectly:

A child talks in the language of gesture
   and he thinks in the language of images and emotional recall.
He understands speech but not so much the words themselves as the gestures
   and tone of voice.[35]

Children's sensitivity to tone and gesture means that we need to be highly aware not just of what we say to them but of how we say it. Perhaps our tone of voice actually reinforces a negative message that they have received elsewhere, for example, at school. Interestingly, some of the children most adept at picking up vocal cues are those who live in abusive situations where their survival depends on anticipating the mood of the parent and knowing how to react accordingly. Perhaps Shanice has learned that keeping herself to herself, being as quiet as a mouse and not engaging with her surroundings, is a way of avoiding being noticed and picked on at home.

Modelling

As a child in Sunday school, I learned a song beginning, 'What you are speaks so loud that the world can't hear what you say.' Whatever we may think of the song, it illustrated modelling. The child's first role models are family members, and children will 'do what I do' rather than 'do what I say'. If Kate sees that Mum always gets Dad to give in by bursting into tears, she will adopt the same tactic to get what she wants. If big brother Kevin has learnt to play off Mum against Dad to get what he wants, sooner or later little sister Kate will do the same. Cassie has obviously discovered that sulking produces the desired results.

Beyond the family, role models come from a wide variety of sources. Children pick up language, attitudes and ways of behaving from mates at school or on the street. Marketing adverts and promotions provide very powerful role models. Lisa, who is five, wants to dress like Barbie, have the beautiful make-up and hair kit that Barbie has, and have her room decorated Barbie-style. Television is a principal source for role models, good and bad. Children brought up on soaps may assume that normal family life is about dropping in and out of relationships, violence in the home, betrayed confidences, and rebellious teenagers. They may also see loyalty, positive friendships, and loving—if somewhat chaotic—

family lives, depending on what programmes they watch. Pop stars and bands provide very powerful role models (hence the popularity of programmes such as *Pop Idol* and *Fame Academy*), as do football stars. The money, status and personality cult associated with celebrities are hugely attractive to children and young people. Increasingly, the Internet is giving the message that anything is available and accessible: we can do our homework online while we chat to our friends; we can play games, download music and create pictures. Life without computers is inconceivable to children.

The power of the messages received through modelling is all the greater because we tend to be unaware of them. We are constantly exposed to them in everyday life, to the extent that we think it is 'in one ear and out the other'. We fail to appreciate that constant exposure to and repeated hearings of such messages can have a very powerful impact on impressionable and vulnerable children.

Commands

Commands are also a powerful source of script messages for children. 'Don't cry!' 'Stop fidgeting!' 'Don't touch!' 'Shut up!' 'Go away!' If said often enough in a harsh, critical tone of voice, the child will take in the message behind the command. 'Don't cry!' may mean, 'Don't show your feelings' or 'Crying is for wimps.' 'Stop fidgeting' can mean, 'It's not all right to be a child; the sooner you can be like an adult and sit still, the better.' 'Don't touch' can mean, 'It's not all right to be inquisitive, to be interested in things.' 'Shut up' can mean, 'It's not all right to express your needs.' 'Go away' can mean, 'I wish you weren't here', or even 'I wish you'd never been born.' It is very easy to snap a command at a child without thinking about the unspoken message behind the words, and what this message can do to the child's sense of self or her self-esteem. Kyle's fluent use of commands ('Geroff!') and expletives may well reflect the messages he hears at home or the programmes he watches on television.

Attributions

Sit next to a family in MacDonald's and listen. 'You're messy!' 'You're clumsy' (as the child knocks over the drink). 'You are stupid!'

'She is bawling, blubbering, whining again!'
A bouquet of words which adults invented for use against children.[36]

A steady diet of negative attributions can become a self-fulfilling prophecy. If a child hears often enough that she is stupid or clumsy, she will come to believe it and will grow up to be clumsy or stupid. If a child hears himself referred to often enough in the third person as 'a little troublemaker', he will come to believe this of himself. Kyle's mother constantly spoke about him in this way to others—in front of Kyle. She was a deeply caring mother, but was at her wits' end with him and would constantly seek advice from others in front of him. This child heard himself referred to as 'a nuisance', 'a pain in the neck', or 'a handful'. Little wonder he came to take on board these messages as part of his life script. We also liken children to others: for example, 'You're just like your cousin Tom.' If cousin Tom is a popular member of the family, this may be a positive message for the child, but if cousin Tom is an embarrassment for whatever reason, the child may feel that he, too, is someone to be ashamed of.

Trauma

The experience of trauma in the life of a child can result in the child's taking in very powerful, long-lasting messages that may be very negative, and the earlier the trauma occurs, the more profound will be the effect. Experiences such as loss, the death of a parent or close relative, severe illness, a hospital stay, abuse, neglect and (on a wider scale) war, natural disaster or violence are deeply shocking and terrifying for a child. They can destabilize natural developmental processes. A child may take on board that she has caused the loss, death, illness or abuse and that she is therefore at fault, worthless, sinful and dirty. She may take in a message that she is unlovable, unwanted, or that she should never have been born. She may come to believe that the world is dangerous, all adults are cruel, that God does not exist or certainly does not care.

Positive messages

Finally, the child may also receive positive messages. Verbal and non-verbal messages, modelling, commands and attributions can be positive as well as negative. A child may grow up experiencing congruence between the verbal and non-verbal messages, such that positive words are matched by a positive tone. A child may experience positive, appropriate role models, with care-givers filtering out those they perceive to be harmful or unhelpful. Commands and attributions may be respectful and enriching: 'Please help me to do this'; 'You are such a lovely child.' Most children will experience a mixture of positive and negative messages, but a steady diet of positive messages will enable a child to develop a positive script.

An awareness on our part of the types of messages children have received as they have grown up, and therefore an understanding of how the life script—the child's way of understanding the world— has been formed, are essential if we are to be effective in helping to nourish children's spirituality.

PART THREE

Damaged spirituality

We have explored the qualities within the child that go to make up his or her spiritual birthright, and we have seen that on to these qualities is stamped the impression of the messages the child receives from care-givers and the environment as he or she grows up. These messages, the child's perceptions of them and the child's experiences together create the life script. What, then, is the interaction between the child's spirituality and the messages that are received—the inner and outer worlds? How do the two relate? The task of the child as he or she grows up is to make a 'good fit' between the inner and outer worlds of experience. Children need to make sense of these two worlds, to discover how to integrate them, but often the messages received run counter to or negate inborn spirituality.

From the day she is born, the child's spirituality begins to be damaged. In some instances, this can even happen from the time of conception. Research shows that the baby in the womb is very sensitive to movement and sounds from the 'outside world'. If a mother is living in an unhealthy, dysfunctional setting, the baby may well hear sounds of anger and violence or experience sudden rough, destabilizing movements that can damage his emerging core sense of safety and of self. He is taking in non-verbal messages about unpredictability, uncertainty and lack of safety, which will become held in his body memory and can contribute to damaging his sense of trust.

The experiences a child has, the messages received from care-givers, peers and the environment, and a child's own perceptions of these experiences and messages, all contribute in various ways to crush, rubbish, clutter, negate and thus damage inborn spirituality. How does this happen? Look again at the child's spirituality—spontaneity, imagination, gentleness, joy and wonder, sense of adventure, candour, trust, resilience, innocence, giving hearts, and so on. The crucial point to note is that it is not just 'bad' or 'inadequate' parenting that damages children's inborn spirituality: it is something we all do as adults, often without being aware of it.

Openness

Parents and other care-givers will often put their own interpretation on the ways in which it is appropriate for a child to be open to the world. 'Hurry up!' 'Don't touch, that's dirty.' 'Don't be silly, it's just a leaf.' 'You naughty boy, now look what you've done!' 'No, we haven't got time to look at that.' 'I told you, leave it alone!' Such comments are just the beginning of encouraging a child to shut down his or her open spirit. So children learn to repress their curiosity and begin to lose the ability to see wonder in the world. How often, for example, do we choose the easiest options when it comes to occupying children? It takes less effort to buy a child a new game or a new video to watch than it does to play with him or her ourselves, but we then miss out on opportunities to explore how we can nurture the capacity for wonder, excitement, exploration and fun.

While there is nothing wrong with games and videos in their own right, too much television, too many or inappropriate computer games, PlayStations and Gameboys can all clutter a child's ability to find nourishment in simpler activities. The observation is frequently made that when we give an infant a new toy, he or she finds the greatest pleasure in playing with the box.

Children are quickly taught the social conventions about showing feelings: 'Don't make a scene'; 'You mustn't laugh so loudly'; 'Just take the cake nearest you'; '"I want" doesn't get in this house.' After all, our children's behaviour reflects our parenting skills and our values. We discourage children from making their own choices: it is so much easier to do it ourselves or to make the decisions ourselves. I have many recollections of incredulous comments from scandalized adults when our children were small: 'You mean you ask him what he wants for dinner? He should just eat what you give him!' 'You ask her what she wants to wear?' Part of helping children to handle their feelings appropriately is to teach them how to make good choices, so that they can learn to understand the link between the choice they make and the feeling of confidence that it can engender. Learning to say 'no' (and to hear 'no'!) in a constructive way is another way we can help children to handle feelings. We frequently hear children being encouraged not to cry: 'Come on, big boys don't cry!'; 'You are a cry baby'; 'What a wimp!' The message is that it's not macho to show your feelings. As children get older, part of having street cred is to evince a boredom with life, restricting excitement and interest to certain topics.

Many children have their sense of trust damaged from a very early age. They may experience inconsistency, unreliability, insincerity, and a lack of trustworthiness in parents, care-givers and other adults with whom they come into contact. They may find that adults let them down, or that those they should have been able to trust abuse them emotionally, physically or even sexually. Such children quickly learn to shut down, to regard adults with a furtive mistrust, so as to avoid being hurt. But we can also damage openness and trust in other, less obvious ways. We can promise to take a child somewhere or buy them something, and then forget to do it. It is not intentional on our part, but we simply do not remember, or we do not have time, and it is not a priority—to us. To a child, however, it can be devastating, especially when it happens repeatedly.

We can also shut down a child's open, welcoming spirit by criticizing their attempts to join in a conversation in front of strangers, by making them feel small, by telling them to 'run along, we're talking'. We may need to have an adult conversation, but we need to learn ways of giving messages to children that do not damage their confidence and self-esteem.

Immediacy

Damaging a child's ability to live in the here and now can happen through overloading the child with adult responsibilities and cares. A child who has to take on adult roles of caring for younger siblings and helping to run the house, or is used as a sounding board for parental frictions, can find their free spirit crushed. Many children have their simplicity and innocence damaged through witnessing scenes and hearing conversations that are inappropriate. Too many restrictions, rules and boundaries can crush a child's spontaneity. Likewise, too few boundaries can leave a child feeling unsafe, uncared for and floundering. Where parental boundaries are not in place, the child suffers. Often children lose the ability to be fully present because they are weighed down by concerns that they should not have to carry.

Children's simplicity can also be damaged by allowing them to grow up too quickly. Inappropriate television programmes, videos, DVDs and games can clutter their uncomplicated approach to life with visual images that are not helpful. Girls are especially vulnerable in this respect: the five-year-old who wants a crop top, the nine-year-old reading *Sugar*, or the seven-year-old who is asked if she has a boyfriend. There is a fine balance between helping a child to feel confident among her peers, and developing or holding on to home values that may be at variance with those of her peers.

Damaging children's spontaneity is very easily done because a child is easily embarrassed. Their off-the-cuff comment or joke may be inappropriate, the offer to do something may not be needed, but it is how we respond that is crucial in ensuring that we don't make children feel humiliated or rubbish their spontaneity.

Freedom of spirit

You say 'He ought to… I want him to…'
And you look for a pattern for him to follow
And you search for a life which you wish him to have.[37]

As adults—parents and care-givers—we walk a fine line between giving a child a path to follow and setting him free to follow his own path. We damage spirituality when we surround a child with too many 'You ought to… you must… you should…' instructions. Likewise, we damage it when we do not put boundaries in place, because a child needs boundaries to push against in order to grow. Without boundaries, children feel unsafe.

Many children do not have enough opportunities to allow their creativity and imagination to have free rein. Lack of private space can be a limiting factor. Because parents are concerned about child protection issues, children cannot go off and be alone in their own space as they used to, but free play is crucial to the development of a child's imagination. A child also needs friends with whom to laugh, argue, cry, dance, build, explore and do countless other tasks. Again, it is easy to rubbish the importance of play by our attitude. We may dismantle a carefully built 'castle' because it is in our way, or throw away a bunch of dead flowers without a second thought. We may brusquely interrupt a child's description of a 'journey' he went on because his description is lengthy and confused and we have more important things to do. We may enter a child's room without knocking, although she has shut the door and clearly wants to be private. A child whose own space is not respected will not learn to respect others' space. In the same way, a child whose possessions are not respected will not learn to respect others' possessions.

At the core of each child's spirituality is the need to be loved. Each child needs to know that there is someone there for him or her unconditionally. Unfortunately, many children suffer core damage to their spirituality because they are not loved or are loved conditionally. The message some children hear again and again in commands such as 'Get lost' or 'Get out of my sight' is, 'I wish you were dead or had never been born', whether it be direct or indirect. The message other children hear is, 'I'll love you if you're good', 'I'll love you if you'll do what I want', or 'I'll love you if you'll keep our secret'. Conditional love is not real love; it is self-centred love on the part of the adult. A baby in arms will sense if he or she is not loved and not wanted, and this means that the core sense of self is at risk.

Henri Nouwen powerfully reminds us how important the knowledge of God's love was in Jesus' life. Speaking of Jesus' baptism, he says, 'It was then that he heard that voice deeply entering his heart: "This is my Son, the Beloved, my favour rests on him" (Matthew 3:17). That voice carried him through life and shielded him from bitterness, jealousy, resentment, and revenge.'[38] Similarly, a core sense of being unconditionally loved will carry a child through all the experiences of his life.

The image of God is damaged

So the image of God in the child, what Korczak calls 'the white, bright holiness of childhood', becomes marred, tarnished and scratched. These three words have slightly different connotations, and each refers to a different aspect of the damage that impacts the child's spirituality. First of all, inasmuch as each child is a part of our fallen creation, he or she cannot help but be marred by the sin that has touched the whole human race: 'All people were made sinners as the result of the disobedience of one man' (Romans 5:19, GNB). In other words, there is a bias towards sin in every child, which is there from the moment of conception.[39]

Second, from the moment of birth, the image of God in the child becomes tarnished by the impact and influences of the surrounding world. The word 'tarnished' is often associated with silver, which becomes discoloured and blemished when exposed to the air. An image that is reflected clearly in a freshly polished, shining spoon becomes faded and mottled when the spoon gets tarnished. Eventually it may be impossible to see the reflection at all. In the same way, the 'air' surrounding the child is full of influences, values, expectations and norms that come from the family, the community, the media, the culture and so on, and the child cannot help but be exposed to them. Some of them may keep the image of God bright, but others will tarnish it.

Third, as the child grows up, the image of God will be scratched by both the deliberate and the inadvertent messages that are given and received. Because this type of damage is more specific and targeted (even when unintended), it can result in a 'scratch' on a particular aspect of the child's spirituality—on trust, for example, or on the expression of feelings.

The power of shame

We noted above that in order for children to develop as whole, integrated people, they need to make a 'good fit' between their inner and outer worlds. How a child feels and perceives his or her self needs to be accepted, recognized, valued and (ideally) celebrated by the outside world. If this does not happen, if the outside world is not broadly receptive, then a sense of shame will develop in the child.

Shame is the experience that what is me is not acceptable, that this is not my world. As such, shame signifies a rupture (or threat of a rupture) between the individual's needs and goals on the one hand and environmental receptivity to those needs and goals on the other. [40]

An understanding of shame and the powerful influence it can exert on the child is crucial to an understanding of the way in which the child copes with the experience of rejection from the outside world. In order to make sense of this rejection, children will adjust the boundary between themselves and the world outside, such that 'the need that is not received by the other is disowned and made "not me"'. [41] In their book *The Voice of Shame*, Robert Lee and Gordon Wheeler note that we all at times experience shame at a low level, where our attempts to connect with another might be rejected or not understood. We respond by feeling shy, embarrassed or uncomfortable, and so we withdraw. We may then make another attempt to reach out in a different way, or find ways of making the 'world out there' more responsive. Where the sense of rejection is deeply felt, however—perhaps where the core sense of 'who I am' is already damaged through experiences of abuse or loss or negative messages of being unwanted or not valued—the child will respond in one of three ways: (a) he will disown the need; (b) he will lose a voice for the need; or (c) he will develop coping strategies to compensate for the rejection. Although set out here as three distinct stages, in reality they are interconnected.

Disowning the need

If children repeatedly find that something they need and long for is not provided, or that their attempts to obtain it are rejected, they will eventually come to disown the need altogether, and will treat it as something they do not need or want—something that is 'not me'. Take, for example, young Alfie, who needs and longs for loving touch. His mother is a single mum, stressed, with younger children and many financial worries. She had no time or inclination to spend time cuddling him as a babe in arms. As he gets older, she tells him not to be so 'soft', or she ignores him as he wants to rub his cheek on her arm, bury his face in her lap or put his arms around her. He feels pushed away. He sees that no one else in the family expresses feelings in this way. As this need is ignored, or he feels shamed or embarrassed whenever he tries to get the need met, Alfie will soon decide that neither does he have this need. He disowns it.

Losing a voice for the need

As Alfie continually disowns this need, he will eventually 'lose a voice' for it: in time, he will no longer know how to ask for loving touch. He may even lose awareness of it. In your club, Alfie may well be the child whom you feel you can never get close to—the child who seems to surround himself with a defensive wall. However, although awareness of the need may disappear, the need itself will not, and he will be left with a sense of worthlessness, inadequacy and/or isolation. 'Any time it emerges (awares or unawares), the person experiences shame in order to continue the perception of the need as "not me" and in order to live in harmony with an environment perceived as not supporting or accepting the need.'[42]

Coping strategies

Once shame becomes so much a part of the person that it comes into play automatically, and he loses a voice for the original need, it is very difficult to access the need. So it is very hard for Alfie, who now no longer even seeks or asks for loving touch, to access the need and even to be aware that he has a need in terms of his relations with others. Instead, he will develop coping strategies to compensate for the disowned need. So, for example, because his need for touch is not met positively, he may seek to have it met negatively. He may become the child who is constantly hitting, poking and pushing other children. Alternatively, he may seek for touch in inappropriate sexual ways. He has developed these behaviours as his coping strategies, albeit unconsciously.

One child therapist has described coping strategies as 'water wings': as the child swims across the pool of experience from childhood to adulthood, so his water wings help him to survive. Often we want to remove the water wings, to tell the child that this is not the way to 'be' with others. However, to do this is to remove the strategies he has developed for survival. To do it without providing other strategies—without first teaching him to swim—will mean that he drowns.

Gordon Wheeler describes these coping strategies as 'creative adjustments' and suggests that they serve, in an indirect way, to meet some of the child's needs so that some level of growth and development may still go on. This is particularly so in the case of a child who, for example, has had to grow up too soon, perhaps caring for younger siblings or even for an ill or inadequate parent. Such a child may have developed 'water wings' or 'creative adjustments', such that although she has lost her voice for her own needs—her need to play, to have time and space for herself, to simply be a child—she is nevertheless very able to meet the needs of others. She may come across as mature, capable and organized. As a result, we may miss seeing that she is also very passive, adaptive and emotionally shut down. The children we tend to be most concerned for are those who are 'in your face':

... the ones who are the most disorganized, whose affective, cognitive and behavioural worlds (like their outer worlds, invariably) are disconnected from each other and poorly articulated in themselves so that behaviour is random and reactive, disconnected from the inner world of wants and needs or the outer world of satisfaction and possibility. [43]

Shame is about relationship: we feel shame in relation to other people and, as we will see in the next section, it is only through relationship that healing can begin to take place.

A fragile creation

Have you ever played Jenga or Ta-ka-ra-di? This is a game of skill in which small wooden blocks are stacked up to form a tower. Players then have to remove individual blocks carefully, without destabilizing the tower and making it collapse. Because the blocks are not perfectly even, you may be able to slide out a single piece quite low down in the tower without causing it to collapse, but you will have made the whole tower more fragile. A child's spirituality is like a game of Jenga. The earlier in life a child's spirituality is damaged, the deeper the damage will be. A baby who has no experience of a warm, intimate, responsive care-giver, a toddler whose faltering steps to reach out and explore are crushed, a young child who is discovering that adults are inconsistent and unavailable —the damage that occurs in the world of such very young children has the greatest long-term impact. As we saw above, the child's way of seeing the world is formed by the age of seven. When the image of God in the child is scratched during these early years, the impact is profound. As children's workers, we want to be in a position to put a framework of faith around the child's nascent spirituality, but the extent to which the child's innate spirituality has been damaged will affect the ability of the child to move towards faith.

Take a couple of examples. Jamie has grown up on one of the toughest estates in East London. His home environment is soulless. For the whole of his short childhood (he is seven), he has lived in a redevelopment area. First he was surrounded with derelict, boarded-up buildings. Now they have been turned into building sites, 'no entry' sites with dust, mud, noise, heavy machinery and danger signs. Jamie and his mates, being typical streetwise youngsters, know how to get the best out of the derelict buildings, how to squeeze through the corrugated iron fencing to play in the rubble, where the dried-out carcass of the dead rat was, and also where discarded sharps are thrown. It is fun also to watch the JCBs and cement mixers, and see the deep-dug holes fill with water after the rain. The boys also go to the park sometimes, but the older kids always break the swings or throw them over the top bar, round and round so that the little kids can't get them down. The slide doesn't work so well either, because of the spray-paint graffiti all down the slope.

One day, Jamie drops in to his local Sunday group, where the leader is talking about the wonderful, breathtaking world that God the creator has made: mountains and oceans, massive trees, colourful flowers, amazing animals and birds. It sounds really exciting—a bit like one of the holiday places advertised on telly—but obviously nothing to do with Jamie's world. He knows his world. His world is not beautiful. No one has ever shown him anything in his world that could engender a sense of awe and wonder (well... maybe apart from the dead rat!). He finds it impossible to take on board the idea of God as a creator, or of a world that is to be valued and treated with respect.

Natalie is ten, nearly eleven. She lives with her mum and dad in a two-bedroom housing association flat. Natalie has a younger sister and a younger brother. Mum works shifts in an old people's home. Dad's a bus driver, working the night buses. When he's at home in the day he's usually asleep, and Mum's usually at work. Natalie is quite mature for her age and very responsible. She has to be: she's usually the one looking after the younger children. Mum relies a lot on Natalie, and Nat knows not to step out of line. Ever since she can remember, it has been 'Natalie, do this'; 'Natalie, do that'; 'Natalie, here's the list'; 'Natalie, make sure that…'. Natalie has had her whole short life organized for her ever since she can remember. There is never a question: 'Would you rather do this or that?' or 'Which do you think…?' Natalie has never ever been offered a choice. The household might not survive if Natalie made a wrong choice.

In the kids' group at church (where Natalie goes each week), the leader has been talking about making a choice to follow Jesus, about deciding that you want to be his friend. This is like a foreign language to Natalie. What does making a choice mean? How do you make choices? What do you weigh up to decide if it is a good choice or a bad choice? What if you make a mistake? What then? How can a child who has never learned to make her own choices, who has lost a voice for expressing her own wants, whose spirituality in this respect has been damaged, understand what is meant and make an informed decision to 'follow Jesus'?

Both Jamie's and Natalie's spirituality has been damaged very early on. If we want to be effective in helping them to put a faith framework around their spirituality, we need first to repair this damaged spirituality so that it can be used as a springboard to faith. We want to give Jamie some experiences of a creator God, experiences that will help to give a voice to his sense of awe and wonder. We want to help Natalie explore choices—how to make them, what to take into account—so that we can help to give her a voice for her own needs while being sensitive to and respectful of her role in her family. We want to explore the best ways of repairing their damaged spirituality.

NOTES

1   Macrina Wiederkehr, *A Tree Full of Angels* (HarperCollins, 1990), p. xiv.
2   Henri Nouwen, *¡Gracias!* (Orbis Books, 1993), p. 123.
3   Annie Dillard, *An American Childhood* (Harper & Row, 1987), p. 21.
4   *A Tree Full of Angels*, p. 83.
5   David Hay with Rebecca Nye, *The Spirit of the Child* (HarperCollins, 1998), p. 9.
6   *The Spirit of the Child*, p. 10.
7   While there are numerous 'adult' definitions of spirituality, I have developed this definition as embodying characteristics that are distinctive to children.
8   *The Spirit of the Child*, p. 10.
9   Robert Coles, *The Spiritual Life of Children* (HarperCollins, 1992), p. 277ff.
10 Sandra Joseph (ed.), Theresa Prout and Anne Hargest Gorzelak (trans.), *A Voice for the Child: The Inspirational Words of Janusz Korczak* (HarperCollins, 1999), p. 101.
11 *A Voice for the Child*, p. 55
12 Bel Mooney, *Here's Kitty!* (Mammoth, 1992), p. 13.
13 *A Voice for the Child*, p. 75
14 *¡Gracias!*, p. 123.
15 *A Voice for the Child*, p. 24
16 Jerome W. Berryman, *Godly Play: An Imaginative Approach to Religious Education* (Augsburg, 1995), p. 59.
17 *Godly Play*, p. 60.
18 *Godly Play*, p. 18.
19 *A Voice for the Child*, p. 89
20 See Chapter 4, 'A Geography of the Spirit', in *The Spirit of the Child* for a detailed discussion of what comprises these 'categories of spiritual sensitivity'.
21 Alice Miller, *The Drama of Being a Child* (Virago, 2001 revised edition), p. 7.
22 For further discussion around the topic of what a child is, see 'What is a child?' by Kathryn Copsey, in Glenn Miles and Josephine-Joy Wright, eds., *Celebrating Children* (Paternoster Press, 2003).
23 Dawn DeVries, 'Toward a Theology of Childhood' in *Interpretation: A Journal of Bible and Theology*, Vol. 55, Number 2, April 2001, p. 163ff.
24 *A Voice for the Child*, p. 73
25 See Eric Berne, *What Do You Say After You Say Hello?* (Corgi, 1975), pp. 41ff, and Phil Lapworth, Charlotte Sills and Sue Fish, *Transactional Analysis Counselling* (Winslow Press, 2000), pp. 111ff.

26 Anthony Browne, 'Babies socialise within seconds' in *The Observer*, 9 July 2000.

27 *The Drama of Being a Child*, pp. 31–32.

28 Jean Illsley Clarke, *Self-Esteem: A Family Affair* (Hazelden, 1998), p. 270.

29 *Self-Esteem*, p. 35.

30 *The Times*, 17 April 2004.

31 *A Voice for the Child*, p. 15

32 *A Voice for the Child*, p. 12

33 *Transactional Analysis Counselling*, p. 83.

34 *Celebrating Children*, p. 130.

35 *A Voice for the Child*, p. 22

36 *A Voice for the Child*, p. 30

37 *A Voice for the Child*, p. 8

38 Henri Nouwen, *Walk With Jesus: Stations of the Cross* (Orbis, 1990), p. 22.

39 It is important to note that we are not here discussing the issue of accountability before God and at what point a child has an understanding and awareness of it. For a thoughtful discussion of this issue, see *Perspectives on Children and the Gospel* by Ron Buckland (Scripture Union Australia, 2001).

40 Robert G. Lee and Gordon Wheeler, eds., *The Voice of Shame: Silence and Connection in Psychotherapy* (Jossey-Bass, 1998), p. 9.

41 *The Voice of Shame*, p. 9.

42 *The Voice of Shame*, p. 10.

43 *The Voice of Shame*, p. 207.

section two

Restoring the image

PART ONE

A right focus

Whenever we make a relationship with the child on any basis but that of his own individuality, we violate something in his soul.
FRANCES WICKES[1]

In all that has been said so far, there is no attempt to romanticize the child or to look on the child in any sense unrealistically. The spirituality with which a child is endowed comes as God's gift through being created in his image. It is amazing—as are all God's gifts. It is amazing—and it is also damaged.

An upside-down kingdom

The child has a very special place in God's heart and a key role to play in our understanding of the kingdom of God. Has it ever occurred to you that Jesus missed an ideal opportunity in Matthew 18 and 19 to demonstrate what and how we should be teaching children? It would have been such a help to those of us who are children's workers and parents if he had suggested some key areas to teach young children, or given advice on how to handle recalcitrant teenagers. His encounters with children are significant (among other things) for what they do not tell us. He does not show us how to teach, discipline, protect or even evangelize children (although each of these has its place). Instead he twice tells us as grown-ups to change and become like children. Jesus' priorities are not about what we should do *for* children, but about what we can learn *from* children. Jesus turns upside down our grown-up approaches to the world and tells us to approach the world—and him—like children.

So much of Jesus' teaching carries this upside-down dimension. John 3:3 tells us that we cannot see the kingdom of God unless we are born again. Why is this phrase such an issue with many people? It is so logical! If we are to become like children, then obviously we need to start at the very beginning and be reborn. We need to take our first steps under God's watchful eye. 'How can a grown man ever be born a second time?' (John 3:4). Nicodemus was not into Jesus' upside-down kingdom. He had not grasped that he needed to 'become like a child'.

Birth and before

The Bible gives us some key insights into God's heart for us in the earliest moments, hours, days, weeks and months of life, and even before we ourselves have any understanding of what life is. God says to the prophet Jeremiah, 'I chose you before I gave you life' (Jeremiah 1:5, GNB) and in the letter to the Ephesians we read, 'Before the world was created, God had Christ choose us to live with him and to be his holy and innocent and loving people' (Ephesians 1:4). These verses are beautifully paraphrased by Sr Macrina Wiederkehr:

Before I formed you in the womb
you were contained in my being.
I have known and cherished you forever.

Long before the world began,
I was a spark of God's love.
I was already chosen in the heart of God
to be holy, to be dear.[2]

God reveals his love for us through conception, life in the womb, birth and infancy—that crucial period for a child's future development:

You created every part of me; you put me together in my mother's womb…
When my bones were being formed, carefully put together in my mother's
womb, when I was growing there in secret, you knew that I was there—
you saw me before I was born. The days allotted to me had all been
recorded in your book, before any of them ever began.
PSALM 139:13, 15–16 (GNB)

God is intimately involved in our earliest moments. Not only does
he create us with care and perfection, but his eye is on us as we
develop, and his heart of love has plans for our lives—plans that, as
we know from Jeremiah 29:11, are full of hope and goodness.

The Bible gives us another picture of God's love, this time
towards an infant—one who has just learned to walk. Hosea is
speaking of God's love for Israel, and the image he uses is that of a
parent's overwhelming love for a toddler:

I was the one who taught you to walk.
I took you up in my arms.
I drew you to me with affection and love.
I picked you up and held you to my cheek.
I bent down to you and fed you.
HOSEA 11:3–4 (PARAPHRASED)

The child through Jesus' eyes

In my name

What upside-down truths does Jesus tell us about children? First,
he tells us that when we welcome a child in his name, we welcome
Jesus—and not only Jesus, but the one who sent Jesus (Luke 9:48).
Pause for a minute to take this in.

The kids' club is about to begin. The team has prayed together
that it will go well, but first in the queue, energetically kicking the
door, is Darryl. We love him… but our hearts sink. Darryl means

disruption. The upside-down truth of this verse means that as we welcome Darryl, we welcome Jesus. Jesus has a special relationship with Darryl and is there in Darryl. Surely this truth must radically alter our approach to Darryl.

We don't seem to have too much difficulty in taking on board Jesus' teaching about 'whenever you did it for any of my people, no matter how unimportant they seemed, you did it for me' (Matthew 25:40) in terms of someone who is hungry or thirsty or who needs clothing or shelter, but we seem conveniently to forget Luke 9:48 and its application to children. In fact, this is even more powerful than the story in Matthew, in the sense that we are to welcome the child 'in Jesus' name' (GNB). The child carries the status of the ambassador or representative of Jesus, much as a king would send an envoy 'in his name' to speak on his behalf. But children are not conscious of their status; indeed, their very ability to be ambassadors lies in their dependence on the one whom they represent, which is part of the image of God within them. How can we miss such a significant statement about the place of a child in the heart of God?

Infinitely precious

Second, Jesus tells us that children are infinitely precious and valuable. We have already seen the preparation and planning that goes into each life, and the careful precision with which each child is created. Jesus takes this further. Mark records that Jesus was angry with his disciples for turning away the children who were being brought to him (Mark 10:14). This can seem unfair. After all, everyone in Jesus' community knew that the real value of children lay in their potential—what they would 'become' as adults. Childhood was simply a pre-adult preparation time—and girls, of course, were far less important than boys. The disciples clearly saw their role as that of gatekeepers, deciding who Jesus would want to see and who he wouldn't, but they had still not grasped the upside-down nature of the kingdom of God. In welcoming the children, Jesus was demonstrating that he values children for their own sake—for who they are now, not for what they will become. He turned upside-down the accepted way of viewing children. We can picture that he must have thrown the disciples into confusion with his rebuke, as parents and children happily pushed past them in their hurry and delight at Jesus' welcome.

Jesus doesn't stop there, however. He goes on to pass some of his harshest judgment on people who 'cause even one of my little followers to sin'—in other words, on anyone who damages the image of God in the child, damages the child's spirituality. It would be better, he says, to have a heavy stone tied around the neck and be drowned in the deepest sea (Matthew 18:6). This is not a mild telling-off; it is absolutely damning, and shows just how deeply Jesus values children. Stewart Henderson captures this passionate love movingly in his poem, 'And these, all these'.

And if, when I return,
I find just one who has been defiled
One desecrated by your corruption
One invaded by your lust
One chained to your perversion
One burgled of purity
One dominated by your tyranny
One diseased through your indulgence
One famished by your inequity
One reliant on your base favours
One separated from Me through your wicked fancy,
One, who once was Mine
Then I promise
You will never see the sun again
All you will receive is darkness
it will have no end
and you will not know peace
It will be terrible and just on that day
because these, all these are mine.[3]

Loving touch

Third, Jesus demonstrated his loving care to the children through taking them in his arms and placing his hands on each of them (Mark 9:36; 10:16). Again he illustrated the upside-down nature of God's kingdom by taking time to hold, hug and bless *each* child. What an important word to include. Children so often feel missed out and overlooked: Jesus placed his hands on *each* one of them. Physical touch was a significant aspect of Jesus' ministry. He touched the man with the skin disease; he touched the eyes of the blind man; he responded to the touch of Mary caressing his feet; he himself washed the disciples' feet. Jesus knew the importance of fulfilling the hunger for contact, for physical touch. In holding and blessing each child with his love, Jesus reinforced the fact that each child needs the experience of loving, caring touch that blesses and affirms.

Spiritual insight

Fourth, Jesus accepts without question that children have faith—a spiritual insight. Why do we so often miss this or choose to ignore it? Is it because it does not correspond with our adult understanding of what faith is? Maybe we have forgotten that:

They may not have the knowledge we possess,
So the Holy Spirit has to shift much less
In terms of intellectual debris
Than perhaps he might with you. Or you.
Or me. [4]

Jesus speaks about those who cause a child to 'lose his faith in me' (Matthew 18:6, GNB). There is no reason to think that Jesus is talking about children who have some deep understanding of God, and he is obviously not talking about children who have in some way said the 'right words' and entered the kingdom. Jesus' upside-down message, which we need to hear today, is that each child has spiritual insight by virtue of the truth that each child is made in God's image.

This is further reinforced by a wonderful picture painted for us in Matthew 21. Jesus has just caused chaos in the temple by overturning the tables of the money changers and the stalls of the pigeon sellers. Just imagine the shopkeepers trying frantically to retrieve their coins as they rolled across the floor, tripping over the wicker baskets caging the pigeons—the pigeons themselves swooping for the nearest exit, feathers flying everywhere. There would have been noise and hubbub and probably lots of little streetchildren grabbing coins as they rolled behind pillars, under cages, under people's robes.

In the middle of this frenzy, Jesus starts healing the blind and the lame. The religious leaders simply couldn't cope with the wonderful things he was doing; and then, when the children added their voices of praise, it was the last straw. 'Don't you hear what they are saying?' they demanded, pointing at the little urchins as they ran and danced, hopping from one leg to another. Jesus should tell them off! What did children know? How dare they talk about Jesus being David's son? You can just imagine Jesus' serene response and mild amazement as he turned the tables on them, quoting from their own scriptures. 'Yes, I do,' he said. 'Don't you know that the Scriptures say, "Children and infants will sing praises"?' (Matthew 21:16).

I don't imagine that the children paid any attention to this exchange. If they did hear, they probably didn't understand it. They were just having fun, milling around Jesus in the hubbub of the temple. I imagine they had intuited and experienced that here was someone who, unlike virtually every other adult they had encountered in their short lives, really loved and enjoyed being with children. Maybe some of them had been among the children Jesus blessed, as recorded in Matthew 18. But this did not stop Jesus from pointing out to the religious leaders the significance of what the children were saying. How often do we discount a child's response because we question whether the child 'really understands' what he is saying? 'Ignorant children can speak truly about Jesus because God has given them this insight and opened their mouths.'[5] How much do we, as adults, really understand the statements of faith that we make?

Angels with access

Jesus tops off his upside-down teaching about children and the kingdom of God by cautioning us against despising or looking down on any of these children from our lofty and knowledgeable position as adults. 'Don't you know,' he says, 'that their angels are always in the presence of my Father in heaven?' (Matthew 18:10, GNB) or, as the NIV expresses it more graphically, 'always see the face of my Father in heaven'. The Living Bible paraphrases the words: 'I tell you that in heaven their angels have constant access to my Father.' This verse is often overlooked when we explore Jesus' insights about children.[6] Perhaps this is because Christians from certain traditions do not feel very comfortable with the role of angels, but Jesus clearly and unequivocally speaks of children having angels in heaven who are there on their behalf. Although their precise role is not defined, from the context we can imagine that they are relaying back to the Father the ways in which the child is being treated. They are telling him how the child is developing; they are advocating on the child's behalf. They have been charged with the special mission of monitoring the progress of each child, and they bring this progress continually before the face of God in heaven.

The parable of the lost sheep in this context seems to imply that the angels have a special role in ensuring that none is 'lost'. Perhaps we can understand this as meaning 'damaged' in the words of the poem by Stewart Henderson: desecrated, invaded, chained, burgled, dominated, diseased, famished, and therefore separated from the

Father. There are many verses that speak of adults having guardian angels (Psalm 34:7; 35:5–6; 91:11; Isaiah 63:9), but only children appear to have angels who have continual access to God's very presence. This profound truth must surely serve to reinforce just how central is the place of children in the kingdom of God.

Become like a child

Above all, Jesus teaches us the ultimate upside-down truth that if we are to enter the kingdom of heaven, we are to change and become like a child (Matthew 18:3). By implication, we are to discover how to become like them; we are to learn from them in their humility and vulnerability. We are to reflect the qualities of openness, immediacy and freedom of spirit as outlined in the previous section. The fact that this was radical teaching for the Jewish community in Jesus' day is clear, but it is also revolutionary teaching for us today. We may live in an era and a community where we have a much more informed understanding of the developmental needs of children, where 'childhood' as a valid developmental stage is recognized and valued, where children's rights are high on the agenda, where we have the 'Year of the Child', where we appoint a Children's Commissioner—but we still understand very little about the centrality of the child in the teaching of Jesus.

Why is this centrality not reflected in the way we, as Christians, view children within our homes, within our fellowships, within our worldview? We can understand why children are not valued, are dismissed, or are looked down on in so many parts of the world, but given Jesus' teaching on children and his bald statement that unless we change and become as children we will never enter the kingdom of heaven, why do we Christians apparently totally ignore it at all levels? There is very little teaching in our churches, our theological colleges, our ministerial training or our children's work training about what it means in practice to change and become like children.

Our adult perspective

The reality seems to be that we approach every aspect of our world from an adult perspective, and are unable or unwilling to accept that we have anything significant to learn from children. Certainly, we have the right intentions in valuing children, protecting them and recognizing their spirituality, but too often it goes no further. We give the nod to Jesus' teaching that we should turn around and become like children, that we should welcome children in Jesus' name, and that all children have a faith, but there are very few sermons preached on how these truths might impact us. There are few courses at theological colleges on the difference such teaching should make to the way we 'do' church, the place we accord children, or what it really means to 'set a child in the midst'. Little is taught about the staggering truths that God contains each child as a spark of love in his being before life even starts, that conception and bone-by-bone creation in the dark fertility of the womb, and then birth itself, bring into the world a child made in God's image— a child with a knowledge of divine secrets. It would appear that within a Christian orthodoxy that claims to be biblically based, there is an entire strand of teaching in both the Old and New Testaments that we simply choose to ignore.

It is beyond the scope of this book to explore how these insights should impact our understanding of our faith, of the church and of theology in the broadest sense. Such an exploration is about developing what Keith White, Haddon Willmer and others engaged in the process would call 'Child Theology'. In his keynote paper for the Archbishops' Council's Strategy for Children Forum (10 March 2004), Keith White says:

Child Theology is a global process working to inform, engage with and challenge the full range of Christian theology, inspired by Jesus when he placed a little child in the midst… You will notice that it is not a theology of child or childhood; nor is it children's theology. Taking our model from the action and words of Jesus, Child Theology is seeking to re-examine the heart of theology, church and mission, with a view to establishing how different it all looks with a child standing continuously in the midst…

Such theology must be done in context, and a significant aspect of context is the changing world of childhood, and the conditions in which Christians are operating as they relate to children whether in families, churches, playgrounds, schools.[7]

A child-centred attitude

This is the point where we as children's workers come in. If we are to take Jesus' teaching seriously and act on it, then we need to develop a 'child-centred attitude' in our work with children. The choice of the word 'attitude' is deliberate. We can begin by learning what constitutes the attitude, but, in order for it to be genuine, it needs to become a part of us. It cannot be a piece of clothing that we wear when we are with children, then remove when we are among adults. It has to be within our heart. A child-centred attitude is about setting the child in our midst (like Child Theology), and is about seeing the world from the perspective of the child. It does not mean that we deny our adult perspective, but it does mean that we allow it to be challenged, enriched and altered by the perspective of the child. It means that when we are with a group of adults and hear them speaking disparagingly about children, discounting them, or referring to them in a belittling way, we are immediately ready to put an alternative point of view or an alternative construction on the situation. We are there as an advocate for the child, even when no child is present.

How do we develop and nurture a child-centred attitude? There are a number of ways. First, we need to re-examine and challenge our theological understanding of the place of the child within the kingdom of God. We need to recognize that, for too long, mainstream theology has seen children as marginal at all levels—in writing, in teaching, in training, in preaching, in church. We need to approach our work among children using our minds, just as we would other areas of our faith. We need to know what we think and believe about children, their spirituality and their faith, and why we think and believe it.

Second, we need to revisit our own childhood. We need to recall what we were doing at various ages, what we were like, how we felt, how we responded. If our childhood was painful, we need to identify why this was the case. If our childhood was so painful that we have blocked parts off, then we may need to consider receiving some professional help to enable us to explore, understand and come to terms with those parts.

The world of children today is very different from the world in which many of us grew up, and we need to be aware of the changes. We also need to remember that while the context may have changed, the feelings engendered may be the same: excitement, enjoyment, space, fear, being cold-shouldered, jealousy, feeling put down and so on. Sometimes there may be a particular age group that we find really difficult to relate to. The events of our own childhood at the same age may give us a clue as to why this is so. I found the early teenage years of my daughter very difficult: it was hard to think myself into her world. When I was 12 and 13 myself—a crucial time in developing a sense of identity and being a part of a peer group—I was uprooted from my home, my school and my network of friends, and moved to another country and a foreign culture. I changed country, culture, neighbourhood, home, school and friends in the space of one month. The impact was enormous and extremely painful to my fragile emerging sense of self. Little wonder I found it difficult to cope with my daughter's responses. I had yet to cope fully with my own.

Third, we need to enter the world of children today. There are many ways to do this. As parents, that world is thrust upon us, but we can choose not to enter it. In entering, we make ourselves vulnerable and open to change. Try watching a children's television programme with children present. Don't watch it on your own. See what children laugh at, and when they get bored. Note their response to adverts. Follow their process of thought association. What tangents do they go off on to? How do these expressions parallel yours? What foods do they want to snack on while watching telly?

Try playing a game with a child. What are the issues around choosing the game, playing fair or cheating, taking turns, winning? How do they vary depending on age, or on the child's background? At what point do you decide that it is important for the child to win, or for you to win?

Try reading a children's book, magazine or fanzine. What are kids' favourite books these days? What is read at school? Do your kids read at all? Why are magazines such as *Bliss* and *Sugar* so popular? Which age group mainly reads them? What issues are being discussed? How do such issues relate to the topics covered in the kids' work you do with this age-group? Find out about football teams, footballers, bands, pop stars, or wrestling. Watch programmes such as *EastEnders*, *Neighbours*, *Hollyoaks*, *Big Brother*, *Pop Idol*, *Fame Academy*, *WWF*, and other currently popular soaps and TV programmes. The list is endless!

If you really want to immerse yourself in the world of children today, one of the best ways is to volunteer as a classroom assistant or a lunchtime supervisor. Children's culture changes very quickly. When both my children moved up to secondary school, I found that it was not long before I was out of touch with the world of primary schoolchildren. I didn't know what games they were playing in the playground, what the latest 'in' word was, or the most recent gadget. Helping a few hours a week in a Year 6 class was an invaluable way of keeping in touch. It was also an eye-opener to the tremendous value of non-teaching staff in providing the extra pair of hands, the listening ear or the calming response to support a busy teacher, and in offering time to children, many of whom have little quality time from adults.

Finally, we need to get in touch with our own inner child. This is about refinding and reclaiming our own spirituality, the part of us that is able spontaneously and unself-consciously to celebrate life where it is found. It is about seeing the world through child-like eyes. So often, this dimension of our lives is difficult to grasp.

Instead, we are weighed down by adult cares and responsibilities and the pressure of time.

There are days
when
my adult ways
turn tasteless in my mouth
and the child of long ago
starts
pressing on my soul.

On days like that
I long to touch that child again
and let her take me by the hand
and lead me down
a path that has a heart
and show me all the things
that
I've stopped seeing
because I've grown
too tall.[8]

Getting in touch with our inner child is about an ability to relax, have fun and allow ourselves to live in the moment. 'The ability to play and be creative are essential personal and professional requirements.'[9] This was written about child therapists, but it can equally be applied to those who work with children in any capacity. Some of us adults need to relearn—or perhaps learn for the first time—how to play.

PART TWO

Repairing damaged spirituality

Let's pause and take stock of where we have been. We ended the last section by recognizing that if we want to use children's spirituality as a springboard to faith, we need first to repair it where it has been damaged. In this present section, we have thought about the biblical perspective on children and entered Jesus' upside-down value system represented in the kingdom of God, which begins with Jesus' injunction that we must change and become like children. We have thought about how we prepare ourselves for this challenge by developing a new perspective—a child-centred attitude—toward the world in general and to children in particular.

The key role of relationship

Where do we begin in the challenge of repairing damaged spirituality? We need to go back to the very beginning again by taking another look at Genesis 1:26. God did not say, 'Now I will make humans, and they will be like me.' No, he said, 'Now *we* will make humans, and they will be like *us*.' Just as the essence of God is relationship—Father, Son and Holy Spirit—so by virtue of being created in God's image, we too are created as relational beings. We are created to be in relationship with one another and ultimately with God through Jesus Christ and the Holy Spirit. This is of fundamental importance, particularly in terms of our work with children.

Why is it that so much of our reformed theology seems to have moved away from this core relational basis and latched on to a doctrine of individualism? The mainstream Western Protestant Christian tradition in which I was raised was highly individualistic. I was taught that my eternal salvation depended on my individual response to God. It was a response that I had to make myself, individually, personally, even privately. Verses such as Philippians 2:12 (in the Authorized Version) were quoted to me: 'Work out *your own* salvation with fear and trembling'. Although we were encouraged to be part of a church, a community where an understanding of God could be experienced and worked at in relationship with others, the essence of faith was about something very private and inward: myself and God. Many traditional hymns are very individualistic: 'Blessed assurance, Jesus is mine'; 'In a love which cannot cease, I am his and he is mine'; 'Rock of ages, cleft for me, let me hide myself in thee'. It was possible to divorce my relationship with God from my responsibility to the 'world out there' and sit in my religious cocoon, secure in my understanding that God and I were doing just fine, thank you, so I didn't need to bother taking other people's issues on board.

It is not too far removed to suggest that some of our churches are like this—a cosy clique that does not engage relationally with anything outside that might challenge our individualistic comfort zone.

The development of the self through relationship

Some parallel insights in this area come from the psychological therapies—for example, as noted by Gordon Wheeler in *The Heart of Development: Gestalt Approaches to Working with Children, Adolescents and their Worlds*:

This position [the doctrine of individualism] rests on the assumption that something called 'self'—or the essential individuality of a person—

already exists in a real way prior to and apart from relationships and development in a relational field. So deep is this underlying assumption about our nature and our self-experience that it amounts to a dominant cultural paradigm in our thinking and attitudes about ourselves and others; an implicit belief system that colours our language and our experience itself in ways of which we are not at all always fully aware.

Wheeler goes on to extend these insights to our work with children, pointing out:

We sense intuitively that there is something wrong with this picture, some way in which the assumption of 'self before relationship' misses our self-experience of being constituted in and by relationship. To be sure, we have... some clear sense of being a unique locus or synthesis of experience; and certainly that uniqueness is in some way related to our ideas and our sense of self.[10]

If we unpack this, we see that Wheeler is not saying that there is no such thing as the self; rather, he is challenging the traditional Western assumption that the self can exist in a real way apart from relationships. Our self is 'constituted in and by relationship'. Increasingly, recent research on newborn infants is highlighting their ability to recognize and respond to faces in the minutes and hours after birth. Lynne Murray, Professor of Developmental Psychology at Reading University, says:

Infants are motivated to engage with other people from the moment they are born. There is a wired-in programme to help babies lock into those that are caring for them... Babies in the womb learn a lot about their mother's voice—they prefer the sound of their mother's voice over others immediately they are born. Also, from the amniotic fluid they get to prefer the smell of their mother and taste of the breast milk.[11]

Listen to this wonderful encounter between Ethan and his parents.

Within a minute and a half of birth, Ethan is watching his mother intently, scanning the details of her face. He starts grimacing if he is disturbed. But as his mother talks to him, his face becomes more mobile and expressive, showing his pleasure. When his father starts talking, he turns to look at him, and then stares back at his mother when she replies. When his father picks him up, he concentrates on his face, and is thoroughly absorbed, exploring every detail. His father John sticks his tongue out. Ten seconds later Ethan responds, sticking his own tongue out. John opens his mouth wide. A few seconds later, Ethan opens his mouth wide. Ethan, the master mimic, is just 15 minutes old.[12]

Conversely, as we saw above, where a child is raised in isolation with no opportunities for relationship with care-givers, as in the 'paediatric concentration camps' of the 1000-bed Romanian orphanages, development is delayed, the children are severely traumatized and any healthy sense of self fails to develop. Children are born programmed to relate, to interact with the world around them.

In his book *The Interpersonal World of the Infant*, Daniel Stern marries up the insights from developmental psychology and psychoanalytic theory to look at the way in which an infant's sense of self develops. He identifies four different senses of the self, beginning at birth and continuing through the period when a child learns to speak. These senses correspond with significant developmental shifts in the infant, and each describes a different development of the self and of the self in relation to the other. Stern says that there is no confusion between the self and the other at birth or at any point in infancy: infants never have a problem in differentiating what is 'me' from what is 'you'. However, he points out that at each of these developmental shifts:

Infants create a forceful impression that major changes have occurred in their subjective experience of self and other. One is suddenly dealing with an altered person... One could ask, which comes first, an organizational change within the infant or a new attribution on the part of the parent? Does the advent of new infant behaviours such as focal eye contact and

smiling make the parent attribute a new persona to the infant whose
subjective experience has not as yet changed at all?

Stern concludes that it probably works both ways.

Organizational change from within the infant and its interpretation by
the parents are mutually facilitative. The net result is that the infant
appears to have a new sense of who he or she is and who you are, as well
as a different sense of the kinds of interactions that can now go on.[13]

Thus, like Wheeler, Stern recognizes that the self develops through relationship with other people—inter-subjectively—and that this begins to happen from birth. 'My very capacity to know myself arises in an inseparably interactive way with my capacity to know yourself as yourself; each supports, informs and also limits the other.'[14]

I have taken time to highlight these insights regarding the development of the self through relationship because I believe they have profound significance for our work with children at many levels. In the first place, they reinforce the Genesis truth that relationship is at the heart of our being. True, God is one, but it may be argued that his unitary nature arises out of the integration of the three persons of the Trinity rather than from the elevation of one person over the other two. Thus, by being made in God's image, my self, while being unique and distinct because no one else organizes his or her world from my point of view, is also created through relationship because that is how I come to know myself. 'Nothing happens without at least a thread of a relationship.'[15]

Secondly, as we have seen, young children hold the essence of who we are as human beings created in God's image in a way that we, as adults, have lost. They are able to 'hear the voice of God much more clearly' with divine insight.

Thirdly, if this is the case, then their need for and openness to relationships is at the heart of their development at all levels. Their relationship-oriented spirituality has not yet been damaged by the individualism of our Western society.

The enlightened witness

What are the implications of this for the way in which we work with children? Look at 1 Peter 2:6. In building his church, God does not set in place a key doctrine as the cornerstone. He chooses Jesus Christ—a person—thus placing relationship at the heart of his kingdom. In the same way, the cornerstone of our work with children is not what we teach them; it is who we are as leaders, and about the children's relationship with us. Their self is developed through their relationship with us.

Alice Miller, a child therapist, says that each child growing up in an unenlightened, abusive, destructive setting needs what she calls an 'enlightened, conscious witness' in their world—one person who is there for the child and can demonstrate a different way of being. She even goes so far as to say that if Hitler had had one such person in his childhood, he would not have become the manifestation of evil that he did. An 'enlightened witness' is one person who can exemplify a way of being that brings life; a person who can listen to and advocate for a child when no one else does, who can spend time with a child, entering his or her world; a person who can demonstrate that s/he values the child.[16] Korczak describes something very similar:

What a powerful effect on the sad life of a child,
Would be the memory of that person—perhaps the only one—
Who showed kindness, understanding and respect
In a world where cruelty had become the norm.
The child's future life and sense of himself could take a different course,
Knowing there was one person who would not fail him.[17]

Many children in urban areas are living on the margins. They experience dysfunctional family life, inadequate parenting, poverty and abuse at many levels. The parents have themselves experienced little else, and so pass on to their children only what they know. They are not intentionally destructive, but know no other way of being. They themselves need re-parenting.

A local minister described to me the residential holiday weekend their church had run, to which fringe family groupings had been invited. The parents and care-givers had spent the evenings in the pubs and clubs, arriving home later than the children. Discussion—with a total disregard for any children present—had revolved around sexual relationships, promiscuity, incest and rape. When the teenage girls disappeared and no one knew where they were, it was automatically assumed that the worst had happened and they had been raped, when in fact they were just flirting with some new male blood on the beach. Thus the cycle continues from one generation to the next.

There is an extremely powerful psychological force at work here, and often it is only when a parent is made aware of his or her part in the negative cycle, and can come to understand what is happening, that the cycle can begin to be broken. This may be enabled when the parents themselves become aware of what happened to them in their own childhood—and it can happen in any family.

On one occasion when our daughter was six or seven, we had made arrangements to go out for the evening, leaving her with her grandparents. As the time drew near for us to leave, her fear of our going increased to the point that she became nearly hysterical. We were at our wits' end. We spoke later to a friend of ours who was a child therapist. 'What was happening to you around that age?' she asked my husband and me. I recalled that we had returned from Japan to England when I was that age, and I had had to start school for the first time, having been home-schooled up to that point. My most traumatic childhood memory was not wanting to leave my mother at the school gates, and having a no-nonsense headmaster finally bear down on me, pick me up like a sack of potatoes under his arm and carry me screaming and frightened into a classroom, to set me down utterly humiliated with tears streaming down my face in front of a class full of my peers. A traumatic separation experience, to say the least! At the same age, my husband had been sent away from home to school.

'And what happened to your parents at the same age?' my friend went on. My grandmother had died in childbirth when my mother was the same age—an even more traumatic separation. My husband's mother had also experienced separation from her parents at a similar age. Through the powerful unconscious psychological connection between parent and child, our own daughter was in some way picking up the deep separation anxiety that existed across the generations and was re-living it. This, coupled with a very negative early experience of separation at a playgroup that was handled badly, made her feel very unsafe. She couldn't put words to her feelings, but they were so powerful that they threatened to overwhelm her.

Once we were helped to become aware of what was happening and acknowledged our daughter's feelings, the cycle began to be broken. Our friend also suggested that we find a different person to look after our daughter when we were out, someone who didn't carry memories of painful separations, a young person she enjoyed being with. The key issues were that our daughter, without knowing why, was feeling unsafe, and that as we took seriously her feelings we were able to become aware of what was happening and begin to respond by finding ways of making her world a safer place for her, thus breaking the cycle.

Breaking such a cycle may require professional input, but by being there as an advocate for the child, an 'enlightened witness', we as children's workers are in a position to show a different way of being, through our relationship with the child and the family. We can listen, we can empathize with the child, we can enter the child's world and help others to understand the child's feelings, and we can offer a safe place for the child. This places a great responsibility on us to be in the right place within ourselves—spiritually and emotionally. It is a lot easier to offer some teaching or to quote a verse than to 'offer' ourselves, but it is in the relationship with us that the most long-lasting learning will take place.

So our children need a relationship with us, but they will also need a wider experience of positive relationships if they are to develop to their full potential. Let us return to see what we can learn from the psychological theories.

David's world

We noted above, when looking at the development of the self, that while I exist as a distinct self in the sense that no one views the world exactly as I do, nevertheless from birth my sense of self is created through relationships with others. My sense of self and my understanding of other people are created together with the other person as we are in relationship with each other. Because I was created to be in relationship, I was born with a deep need to make connections with the world 'out there'. This is not about making connections with objects, but about connecting with a world of other people like myself. As I relate to other people, so I come to understand and know myself. My 'self' and others are always interdependent.

Moving on from this, it follows that 'understanding someone necessarily includes an understanding of what the world looks like from that person's perspective'.[18] Think about how an infant engrossed in some activity will want the care-giver also to see and enter in, even reaching up to turn her head 'so Mum can see it just as I do'. A child's world is not a world of objects but of people—a world of relationships. A child is born with 'the capacity to notice and relate to the internal experience of others'.[19] But what does understanding another person's perspective mean? It means understanding all that makes that person 'tick'. It means understanding the world or the environment within which that person lives, and how he or she relates to the people, activities and objects in that environment.

In the article just quoted, Robert Lee highlights the importance of this 'relational understanding', which 'flies in the face of our Western individualist tradition'. While he is exploring it from the perspective of developing ethics for one of the psychological therapies, his emphasis on the necessity of understanding the world out there and its interrelationship with the person—the child—is very relevant to this discussion.

We must understand the parts of the environment that the person has made part of him/herself and we must understand the quality of the relationships he/she has with those people/things/activities. We must understand the energy invested and the possibilities for connection and life that such an investment represents.[20]

Take David, for example. We need to know that he is his mum's third child. He is seven. He has two older sisters, one 15, one 14, both by Mum's previous partner. There is constant friction between 15-year-old Jenny and Mum. Jenny can be violent, so much so that Mum can't cope and wants her taken into care. Home life is chaotic because if Jenny is at home, there will be screaming rows, and David, who is Mum's favourite, will often be the butt of Jenny's anger and violence. David comes to club at church each Thursday and Mum will sometimes lend a hand. David takes out his pent-up fear and anger at club, flouting rules and causing disruption. He has no sense of boundaries. When Mum comes to help, he is more manageable, but then all the children are nervous of her strong tongue. It is good to have the extra pair of hands—she knows all the kids—but...

If we want to understand David, we need to enter into relationship with him, so that we understand what the world looks like from his perspective. It is no good simply to tell him off, punish him, or ban him—although some such action may be important in helping to set some boundaries in the short term. A large part of his sense of self has been created through his relationship with his sister, Jenny. As a result, he has made her view of him—as someone to be despised and bullied—his view of himself. This becomes a self-fulfilling prophecy, such that he feels himself to be worthless. Yet he also takes on board his relationship with his mother as her favourite. In his struggle to reconcile these two viewpoints and create his self, he invests his energy in becoming a boundary-less bully at club, while at the same time having a soft, vulnerable side that only emerges occasionally. This is how he has learned to connect with the world out there. How are we, within our church, to support David and effect a change in the way he relates to the world?

The reality is that there are many children in our midweek clubs, our holiday clubs, our Sunday groups and other children's activities who are like David to a greater or lesser degree. We want to break the cycle with such children and see them come through to health. We want to help them break their unhelpful or negative sense of self through positive relationships, and ultimately to discover the most fulfilling relationship of all in Jesus Christ.

Creating a healthy village

There is a saying that 'it takes a village to raise a child'. In other words, a child grows and develops through all the varied relationships within his environment. However, we may borrow a model from one of the psychological therapies, which says, 'It takes a *healthy* village to raise a *healthy* child'. 'This means that proper support for the child includes support for the child's parents as well as for others that relate to the child, that is, siblings, peers, teachers, babysitters, doctors, and so on'[21]—and, we might add, children's workers, Sunday group leaders and ministers. Our churches need to be 'healthy villages' in which to raise children. What does this mean? Lee suggests that there are two core values involved, which I have adapted to the context of the child.

Support for the child

First, children need enough support to develop in healthy directions. Primarily this means that they need to be understood from within their own perspective and from the perspective of the relationships they build. How do we do this? We need to enter the world of the child and see it from his or her perspective: this is true relationship. So, for example, we need to appreciate the way in which David is using his bullying as a means of survival. This does not mean we agree with it, like it or condone it. It does mean that we understand his perspective—where he is coming from. However, we need to help him discover other, more healthy ways of surviving in his world. We need to help him learn healthy ways of relating to others.

We have already looked at the many unhelpful messages that children receive as they grow up. We have seen how a child struggles to make a good fit between his inner and outer worlds, and that where this does not happen, a sense of shame results, causing him to lose a voice for his need, disown it or develop coping strategies. Some of David's shame comes from an inability to make a good fit between his inner world, which longs for positive affirmation from his family members, with his outside world where he receives mixed messages: inconsistency from his mother and violence and verbal abuse from his sister. The shame freezes his ability to grow and develop healthily. He is unable to take in the positive information that we give him about himself, and he is unable to meet and to learn from new situations. What is more, the world 'out there'—his environment in terms of his family—is also unstable and is unwilling to notice his needs or make any healthy connection with him.

Children above all need to be 'seen'. Alice Miller speaks of 'every human being's central need to express herself, to show herself to the world as she really is—in word, in gesture, in behaviour, in art—in every genuine expression, beginning with the baby's cry'.[22] Children need to learn that their feelings about themselves and their world can be *connecting* experiences—relational experiences. When they are not seen, they tend to shut down at core levels. They learn that what is 'me' is not wanted out there. The world out there wants 'me' to be something different, or it may not even want to bother with 'me' at all. So they shut their true feelings inside themselves and stop trying to connect. We might almost say that they retreat back into an individualistic frame of reference, losing touch with their original relational nature made in God's image.

Let me give an example. As a missionary child, I grew up in what was then a very rigid Christian environment. I attended an expatriot school during my teenage years, where virtually all my peers were children of business people or diplomats, living in large houses with personal staff. Socially, I was worlds away from my peer group. I don't recall ever having a friend round to my house through all my teenage years. I was too ashamed: it was so small and my parents were in a different league from my friends' parents. Nor was I allowed to share social activities with my peer group: I couldn't attend dances or go to the cinema.

Because I was not able to relate to my peer group (except at an academic level), that part of me that desperately needed simply to be a teenager growing up was never seen. My feelings in this area never became connecting experiences at home because I couldn't talk about how I felt. The missionary setting was not a safe, non-judgmental place in which to connect. I knew that the Christian worldview would judge me for wanting to do the same things as my friends. As a result, I learned to grow up keeping a whole section of my world, of how I felt, away from my parents, because I learned that these feelings could not be connecting experiences. I was not 'seen' in this area. There was no 'healthy village' in which I could grow up. I also chose to keep my Christian family setting separate from my peers, believing that it would not be understood and would be ridiculed. I could not make a good fit between my inner and outer worlds, so I kept the two worlds completely apart until well into adulthood.

We can give children the experience of being truly 'seen' by how we are with them. I believe that some of the qualities that make a good child therapist are also the qualities we should exhibit in our work with children as Christian children's workers.

- First, we will respect the child. We recall Jesus' approach to children and recognize that we also can learn from children. We also recognize that we need to be there to listen and respond to what is going on in the child's world in an empathic, non-judgmental manner.
- Second, we will be authentic and genuine with children. I must be myself. Children will somehow sense if I am not being real. If I don't know an answer, I say so.
- Third, we will not judge or manipulate. This can be difficult, as we often find it hard to refrain from making judgments, and we can be manipulative without even realizing it. We need to be very aware of our responses to children: the way we phrase questions, the reasons behind the types of activities we choose, even the way we set out a room, all carry messages.
- Fourth, we will be present and in contact with the child to enable our relationship to flourish. This means that we will give the child our full attention, listening and responding appropriately.
- Finally, we will accept the child as he or she is, unconditionally: we will make our best attempt to truly 'see' each child. If we do no more than be this kind of person, then we will have given one of the greatest gifts a child will ever experience. We will have been an 'enlightened witness' for the child.

Support for the setting

The second of our core values is that the field (or the setting) within which the child operates must have support itself if it is adequately to support the child. What constitutes the 'field'? It is the various settings that the child moves in and out of each day: the family, the neighbourhood, the school, the peer group, the clubs, the church.

A key aspect is the family. David's mum is clearly not coping. What kind of support might she need? Help and advice from social services regarding Jenny might alleviate an immediate problem. Perhaps a short break away, or even an evening out, might help to relieve the stress she so clearly feels. Someone taking David out for a day, and a break from Jenny, might give her time to spend with her middle daughter, who seems to be withdrawing amid all the chaos. Even a friendly neighbour cooking a meal for the family might help. Longer-term, parenting classes might be an option.

What are the issues in the neighbourhood that affect the family? Can the church play a role in revitalizing a play area or campaigning for a road-crossing? Can church members play a role in local political initiatives, or do they all live outside the area?

What are the strengths of the school? How much involvement do church members have in activities at the school? Where is additional help needed? Are there Christians on the governing body? Are there dinner ladies (lunchtime supervisors) living out their Christian faith in the playground?

Who are David's friends? Is he part of a gang or a clique, or is he a loner? Are his friends involved in children's activities at the church?

Finally, how healthy is the village that is the church? Where do children come on the list of priorities? When were all church members (not just the children's workers) last challenged about their responsibilities to children? When did the minister last preach about children or focus a service around children? Is there a child-centred attitude within the church as a whole? Do the congregation really 'see' children? Are children's workers highly valued, well resourced and prayed for regularly? Are they recommissioned on a regular basis? Or—much as they love it—are they doing the work, week in and week out, because there is no one else? Are the children 'visitors at' or an integral part of the services and of the life of the church as a whole?

The church must be healthy itself if it is to raise and support healthy children. If David is even to begin to learn what it means to grow up into a healthy young man, feeling seen and valued, and finding a fulfilling relationship with Jesus Christ, he needs the experience of being raised in a healthy church. Based on the foregoing discussion, we can identify five characteristics of a healthy church.

First, it will have a strong focus on relationships. This focus must be modelled by the minister, the vicar, the elders and the church leaders, and then cascade out to the entire congregation. They must take seriously what it means to be made in the image of God. They must recognize that quality relationship is at God's heart, and that real relationships must therefore be at the heart of all that goes on in the church.

This is not relationship at the level of 'Have a nice day'. That is not true relationship, but more like superficial acquaintance. True relationship involves being in genuine contact with another person: it is about seeing and being seen for who we really are. It is not about wearing your emotions on your sleeve; nor is it about deep, intense engagement. It is about having an exchange with someone and coming away feeling really heard and valued. It is about being real and authentic in our contact with others, no matter how brief or matter-of-fact the contact is. It is about modelling the quality of living in the here and now with the other person that we explored above—being present.

Why is it that so few of our churches manage to achieve this quality of relationships? Perhaps it is that we are not willing to give the time needed to work at them. When we ask someone how he or she is, are we really interested or is it just a polite turn of phrase? I have been in churches where I have been asked this question and, when I begin to give an honest reply, I sense the other person glazing over and switching off. They don't really want to know how I am. Do strangers come into our church and feel really touched by the interest, love, acceptance, lack of judgment and lack of backbiting that they find there?

Second, it will be seeking to develop a child-centred attitude. We have seen that a child-centred attitude is one where we are continually aware of the needs of the children in our midst. It is where an awareness of and sensitivity towards children is second nature and informs the way we 'do' church. Families, parents and children will automatically feel welcome and involved. This is not about subordinating the needs of the adult congregation to the needs of the children, or simply making a service 'child-friendly'. It is far more fundamental. It is about taking seriously Jesus' teaching on children and allowing it to penetrate and diffuse through all that we do in our church, from services on a Sunday to weekday activities. It is about how real contact with children will change our way of being church.

Third, it will be a place where children—and adults—are truly 'seen'. It will be a place where our hunger for recognition, for that which makes us stand out in the world, is met, freely and without condition; and where we are known personally by name. It will be a place where our feelings are accepted as authentic, where we can reach out and know that we will be accepted. No matter how much we may be pushed aside elsewhere, we will know that it will not happen in this church. We will have differences but they will not be divisive. Instead, we will celebrate those differences and seek to understand one another's viewpoints.

Fourth, it will be a place where the leadership take time to explore and seriously consider the issues involved in understanding the child as a sign of the kingdom. This is crucial to understanding what we are about in the church. Alongside it is understanding and entering the world of the child. This does not happen by default. Just because I was once a child, it does not mean that I am automatically aware of issues around child development or children's spirituality. In fact, my childhood may have been very traumatic, leaving me with many unresolved issues. We have all experienced damage at some level in our childhood. Unfortunately, most of our theological colleges pay scant attention to any aspects of child development or children's spirituality in their training. In fact, there is little training in any aspect of children's work. Yet biblical teaching on the place of the child is at the very heart of the gospel. 'If you don't change and become like a child, you will never get into the kingdom of heaven' (Matthew 18:3)—not 'you will find it hard to get into...', but 'you will never get into...'.

If we take the broader scope of Child Theology, it 'leads us immediately to reconsider the nature of the kingdom of heaven, creation, anthropology, and the nature of sin and the means by which sin is transmitted through the generations'.[23] This is fundamental to our faith, and surely our responsibility as church leaders and, indeed, Christians, is to begin to explore it.

Fifth, it will be a place where those who work specifically with children, both within the church and in the wider community, are affirmed, valued and supported. I have been in too many churches where the leadership and the adult congregation as a whole have little knowledge of any aspect of the children's work. As a result, the children's workers do not feel valued or supported and they are not adequately resourced. We need to affirm our children's workers in their crucial work; to ensure that they have adequate facilities, resources and training. We need to raise their profile within the church so that they are supported in prayer, and we need to make sure they have time off to rest and reflect. We need to commission them once, maybe twice a year for their work.

We need similarly to affirm others in our churches who work with children in a wider context: teachers, classroom assistants, lunchtime supervisors, social workers, those involved in child protection, residential settings and the courts, and the many others involved at some level with children. They need our prayerful backing.

Most importantly, we need to affirm and support parents in their crucial role in bringing up children. We need to make sure our church structures and activities are family-friendly, that we don't place added burdens of meetings on top of already overstretched parents, and that we plan activities to support and nurture families, single parents, marriages, long-term partners, and others involved in the primary care of children.

Such churches do exist. In fact, I have the immense privilege of worshipping in a healthy church. It would not be considered a thriving church by any of the accepted criteria, such as size, facilities, number of staff, financial viability, education and professionalism, training, leadership potential and so on. It is made up of a group of people, many of whom have suffered or are suffering from mental distress at some level or who have a learning disability. Many in the group know the experience of being marginalized, just as children do. We have very few children in the church, although we have had more in the past, and many of those with learning disabilities approach life with a refreshingly child-like attitude. Yet the church fulfils the basic principles of the five criteria for a healthy church set out above. Just recently a newcomer commented, 'I've never found a church like this before. People really care—they don't mind how you are. They just accept you, no questions asked. And they keep in touch in the week!' I use this example because I want to stress how our understanding of the place of the child is at the heart of all we do as Christians. The child challenges us to look with new eyes at the kingdom of heaven.

I know that I am a child, a child who underneath all my accomplishments and successes, keeps crying out to be held safe and loved without conditions. I also know that losing touch with my child is losing touch with Jesus and all who belong to him. Each time I touch my own child, I touch my powerlessness and my fear of being left alone with no one to give me a safe place. Jesus falls beneath the cross to allow me to reclaim my child... He wants me to discover that beyond all emotions of rejection and abandonment there is love, real love, lasting love, love that comes from a God who became flesh and who will never leave his children alone.[24]

NOTES

1 Frances G. Wickes, *The Inner World of Childhood* (Coventure, 1977 edition), p. 47.
2 Macrina Wiederkehr, *Behold Your Life* (Ave Maria Press, 2000), pp. 23, 26.
3 Stewart Henderson, 'And these, all these' in *Homeland* (Hodder & Stoughton, 1993), p. 88.

4   *Children in the Way* video.
5   Marcia J. Bunge, ed., *The Child in Christian Thought* (Eerdmans, 2001), p. 47.
6   For a discussion regarding the use of the term 'little ones' as applicable to children, see 'The Least and the Greatest: Children in the New Testament' by Judith Gundry-Volf in *The Child in Christian Thought*, pp. 42ff.
7   Keith White, 'Exploring Child Theology', keynote paper for the Archbishops' Council's Strategy for Children Forum, March 10, 2004, p. 10. For further insights into Child Theology and for an inspiring website with a wide-ranging series of articles and news bulletins about children, visit www.childrenwebmag.com. See especially 'Treasure in Earthen Vessels' by Keith White, paper given to the Annual Forum of the Christian Child Care Fellowship, 11 February 2004.
8   Macrina Wiederkehr, *A Tree Full of Angels* (HarperCollins 1990), p. 63.
9   Keith Tudor, 'Integrating Gestalt in Children's Groups', in Gordon Wheeler and Mark McConville, eds., *The Heart of Development: Gestalt Approaches to Working with Children, Adolescents and their Worlds, Vol 1: Childhood* (GestaltPress, 2002), p. 152.
10 Gordon Wheeler, 'The Developing Field: Toward a Gestalt Developmental Model' in *The Heart of Development*, pp. 44–45.
11 Lynne Murray and Liz Andrews, *The Social Baby*, quoted in Anthony Browne, 'Babies socialise within seconds' in *The Observer*, 9 July 2000.
12 *The Observer*, 9 July 2000.
13 Daniel Stern, *The Interpersonal World of the Infant: A View from Psychoanalysis and Developmental Psychology* (Basic Books, 1985), pp. 8–9.
14 'The Developing Field', in *The Heart of Development*, p. 47.
15 Violet Oaklander, 'The Therapeutic Process with Children and Adolescents: A Gestalt Therapy Perspective' in Wheeler and McConville, p. 85.
16 Alice Miller, speaking of Manfred Bieler's book *Quiet as Night: the Memoirs of a Child*, says, 'He shakes off the conventions of the adult world, which rob the child of its right to its own feelings and perceptions by making light of them. Thereby, he becomes its enlightened witness. He is able to do this thanks to a grandmother who sometimes protected him from his parents and by doing so was his helping witness... Many abused children have never had this experience. They therefore have no idea that they would not only have gotten help, but would have deserved it—if only someone in their environment had been a little less heartless, a little less ignorant.' Alice Miller, *Breaking Down the Wall of Silence* (Virago, 1991). pp. 68–69. See also Alice Miller, *Banished Knowledge* (1991), pp. 171ff.
17 Sandra Joseph (ed.), Theresa Prout and Anne Hargest Gorzelak (trans.), *A Voice for the Child: The Inspirational Words of Janusz Korczak* (HarperCollins, 1999), p. 80.

18 Robert G. Lee, 'Ethics: A Gestalt of Values/The Values of Gestalt—A Next Step' in *Gestalt Review 2002*, Vol. 6, Number 1, p. 35.

19 'Ethics', in *Gestalt Review 2002*, p. 37.

20 'Ethics', in *Gestalt Review 2002*, pp. 36ff.

21 'Ethics', in *Gestalt Review 2002*, p. 45.

22 Alice Miller, *The Drama of Being a Child: the Search for the True Self* (Virago, 1997 edition), p. 95.

23 'Exploring Child Theology', p. 5.

24 Henri Nouwen, *Walk With Jesus: Stations of the Cross* (Orbis, 1990), p. 23.

Nurturing spirituality in the urban child

PART ONE

The urban context

In a sense, all that has been written so far is in the nature of a backdrop to what is to follow. We have been setting the scene. But setting the relevant thinking and approaches in place is crucial in terms of what we actually do with children; otherwise, we will find that the doing can become an end in itself. In fact, it is possible to say that if our attitudes and approaches are properly grounded, what we 'do' is almost incidental.

Let us begin by looking at the urban context out of which many children come. Much of what has been said so far is applicable to all children, but I believe it particularly needs to be heard and applied in urban situations—the area of work where my experience lies as part of the CURBS team.[1]

First of all, *where* is urban? 'Urban' can cover a wide variety of settings. It may be the inner city, it may be an outer urban council housing estate, it may be a housing estate in a provincial town, or it may or may not be part of a UPA (Urban Priority Area). At some level, it may even be a little cluster of council houses tucked away on the back road of an apparently affluent village.

Second, *what* is urban? How is urban different to suburban, provincial or rural? We will look at this under a number of headings, and you may well respond, 'But that is characteristic of our area and we aren't what you would call urban.' True, many of these elements can be found elsewhere, but we would argue that often in urban areas there is a greater concentration of these factors over a far wider area than you might find in 'non-urban' areas. Also, there may be fewer positives in the setting to offset the negative effects that such concentration brings.

Environment

Safety

- The concentration and density of traffic is a major concern, especially as most children tend to play on or near streets. Drivers do not always see the ball rolling under the car and are not prepared for the child who follows it.
- Street culture can be another threat and is often linked with violence or crime. To gain or maintain their 'street cred', both boys and girls may adopt macho, hard attitudes and grow up very quickly. Communities of children have slang for the different types of kids found on the street or in their community: townies, pikies, nerds and so on.
- If you are in the right place at the right time, there are ample opportunities to indulge in substance abuse, even for the under-10s, and this provides another opportunity to show that you have street cred.
- Vandalism is a continual issue, ranging from annoying graffiti to serious damage. Bus shelters, churches, shops, play areas, trees, bollards—nothing is immune in a culture where many children do not see their own possessions being respected and therefore do not learn to respect others'. In many places there is an unspoken law that it is all right to damage something that belongs to 'them'—whoever the nameless 'them' might be.
- Broken glass, dog mess, used needles, derelict houses, used condoms, general litter—there is danger in all of these, and even more danger in the unspoken message of 'who cares anyway'. If adults don't bother, then kids certainly won't.
- Poor role models can lead young children into danger. There is often a lack of male role models, and kids will look up to an older child or teenager, who is the recognized group leader, as the model to follow.

Facilities

In many urban areas, the community facilities available may be limited. There may be less variety and fewer shops, leisure facilities or safe play spaces. New ones may open but cannot sustain themselves, and premises are closed and boarded up, which can leave an aura of dereliction and abandonment.

On the plus side, new cultures coming into an area from other countries may rejuvenate a dying locality as new shops, restaurants and places of worship open, offering opportunities to experience a wealth of different foods, clothing and lifestyles.

Space

In inner-city areas particularly, space may be at a premium, both within dwellings, where overcrowding may be a problem, and in the streets, where cars, buses, motorbikes, trucks, pedestrians and roadworks vie for space, resulting in traffic jams, long delays and fraught nerves.

Pollution

- Many urban areas can look tired and dirty as waste spaces and empty corners become covered with litter, and litter bins and dog waste bins overflow.
- Noise pollution is a significant issue, not only in terms of road traffic, but also with trains and airports in some areas. Loud music and raised voices can also contribute.
- Air pollution results from factories and traffic in dense, crowded communities.

Functionality

- Many urban estates were built to be functional with no thought for beauty. Often, materials were cheap and poor quality, so that

30 or 40 years on, communities are left looking bleak, run down and dismal.

- Stairwells, lifts and alleyways become no-go areas peopled by graffiti artists, substance abusers and those who can't be bothered to find a toilet.
- While many local authorities have demolished tower blocks and redeveloped estates, many older estates still exist, with row upon row of soul-destroying concrete blocks and little green space to be seen.

Race

Many children's groups may be enriched by those who come from other cultures and faith backgrounds, but we may be uncertain how to respond to such children. We build good relationships first and foremost by welcoming them and treating them on the same basis as we would any of our youngsters. Most of them were probably born in this country, and, while they may be living in two cultures, they are at home in both. We also build good relationships by taking the time to find out about these other cultures and by getting to know the parents and wider family. We may even want to consider learning the basics of the language of the predominant non-English-speaking community around us—a clear indication that we value and respect our new neighbours.

Above all, we must in no way cause a rift between the child and his home situation by what we do and say. We may not hold to the religious faith of the child's parents, but we must never decry it or tell the child that it is misled or wrong. In point of fact, many children from other faiths come to us with an understanding of prayer, worship, and reverence for that which is holy, of which children from traditional white communities know little, if anything. Children from Muslim backgrounds in particular will have been taught a high respect for Jesus, whom they regard as a prophet and a holy man. This provides a wonderful entrance point for introducing stories from the Gospels.

We may be surprised at having children from other faith communities in our groups, but many such families are very pleased to send their children to groups that have a strong moral and religious basis, and will do so in preference to sending them to purely secular groups. This can only be a positive base on which to build relationships.

Inner cities and other urban areas have experienced a huge influx of newcomers in recent years. While Caribbean, African and Asian communities are a long-established part of our society, more recently we have welcomed incomers from eastern Europe and various parts of the Middle East. The expansion of the European Economic Community has opened the door to other communities. In addition, Britain is host to a large number of asylum seekers, who, particularly in some areas of large cities such as Glasgow, are raising many issues in terms of the provision made for them and the response of the host community.

While many of the older communities have integrated with the traditional white population and live side by side, in other areas the white communities have moved on to outer urban estates, leaving certain inner-city areas to become predominantly Asian, African or whatever the principal populations may be. Thus, outer estates may remain almost exclusively white, while areas nearer a city centre are culturally much more mixed. As the new communities have moved in alongside or have displaced traditional white communities, so issues of resentment have arisen and racist attitudes developed, represented in some areas by the growing strength of groups such as the British National Party. In other areas, the multi-cultural element has created rich and vibrant communities where diversity can be celebrated.

Families

A recent survey conducted among those using the CURBS resources highlighted family issues as being the key concern in their work with children. Many families in urban areas exist under great pressure. This pressure may come from poverty, unemployment, vices such as substance abuse (including alcohol), and issues around promiscuity. There are many reconstituted families, brothers and sisters living in the same family unit who are children of different parents. There may be live-in partners. There may be rapid changeover in family units as partners come and go, leading to a sense of instability among the children. There may be teenage mums with young children, dependent at many levels on the grandmother for support. There is less male involvement in raising children, as it is seen as the woman's job.

Overall, families—even those that are relatively stable—often feel overwhelmed by the pressures that they have to cope with, in the home, in schools and in the community, in raising their children.

Schools

Schools in urban areas face particular issues concerning curriculum and exam requirements that may be far removed from the world of the children, as well as large classes, discipline issues and stressed-out teachers. Teachers need to be able to do far more than simply teach: they need to be counsellors, skilled in conflict resolution, negotiators with and between parents. They need to be a listening ear for overstretched children and parents. They need to have cultural sensitivity, and they need to be able to disentangle which behaviour issues are class-oriented, which are cultural, and which are racial. They need to have an understanding of non-book culture, where a child might have special needs or where family issues might be a significant factor. They also need to be aware of situations in which bullying is taking place, who is doing it and why.

Behaviours

Issues around challenging children also ranked high on the CURBS user survey. We need to be able to identify where behaviours originate. Are they a result of family or personal issues? Are the child's home experiences the cause of behavioural problems? Are they the result of a national malaise, linked with such issues as materialism, consumerism, or sexual promiscuity: 'I must have a mobile phone, a CD or MP3 player; I must have that album; I must have watched this film or video; I must have laid a girl so I can boast to my mates'? Are certain behaviours culturally derived: 'We don't do anything with boys'? Are they a characteristic of our own local community or class-oriented: 'You don't grass on your own'?

Behavioural problems may express themselves through lack of confidence and a sense of low self-esteem, through a lack of ability to concentrate, leading to continuous chatter throughout a class or club, through negative attitudes to authority, or through aggression both physical and verbal because the kids know no other way of expressing themselves. Children may work better on a communal rather than individual basis—in groups. One way around behavioural issues with groups is to get the group leader on board. Many children have a paucity of loving relationships, which again affects the way they can relate to others.

Positive aspects

Our urban communities also have many positive and enriching aspects.

- **They are organic:** Life within an urban community is very different from traditional middle-class living. It is flexible and informal. It has a different approach to time. It is often chaotic, but is real and immediate. It is nearer to the ground and less bureaucratic. Often it goes off at a tangent. It is blurred at the edges, unlike neat, tidy, middle-class life. It is multi-age: often the extended family system still operates.

- **They are constant:** In the middle of all the chaos, there is a deep affection and constancy. A friend will stick by you through thick and thin and will drop everything to help you out in a pinch. And there is wonderful humour, on the street corner, in the pub or launderette, with the kids.

- **They are straight to the point:** There is a ruthless lack of pretension. People are straight: what you see is what you get. There is no middle-class veneer; rather, people will sniff out hypocrisy and a patronizing attitude without concern for your feelings. They say what they think, holding nothing back. They can be hard on you, but you will have no illusions about where you stand.

- **They are communal:** There is a generosity of spirit within an urban community, similar to the old village community—a sense of 'we're in this together'. There is an ease about borrowing from your neighbour if you're stuck, about picking up friends' children from school, about look-ing after next-door's baby while she has to go to the shops. You pop up to the shops in your slippers and hang over the fence talking to your neighbour. The 'community' in terms of a geographic area can also be very small, perhaps a few streets, or a corner of a larger community. A busy road can be a significant barrier, almost a wall, in terms of people crossing over to join the community on the other side.

It is not possible to give a blanket definition of 'urban' that will fit all situations. Urban communities alter rapidly, through population changes as new communities move in, through redevelopment and regeneration schemes designed to improve access, housing and facilities. Even the characteristics above only give a 'feel'; they will not apply in all situations, and others may be more relevant. Nevertheless, all urban communities will doubtless identify with some of the aspects.

What also remains unchanged is that the majority of those living within our inner cities, on outer urban estates, in council or housing association accommodation, or in urban priority areas, are those who are the most marginalized within our communities, those who are the least powerful and the most vulnerable. They are at the 'bottom of the pile' in terms of our society as a whole—and at the very lowest point in these already marginal communities are the children.

Is it just chance that each account of Jesus blessing the children in the Synoptic Gospels (Matthew, Mark and Luke) is followed by the story of the rich man's encounter with Jesus? Jesus welcomes the children in love and states that the kingdom of heaven belongs to those who will receive it like a child. He then looks at the rich man in love, telling him to sell his riches and give the money to the poor to enter the kingdom of heaven. We can clothe this in religious language and interpret Jesus' response to mean that the man must get his priorities straight and not make his riches the most important thing in his life. But Jesus actually tells him to 'sell all you have and give the money to the poor... and follow me'. What a challenge to those of us who are rich, relative to the poverty and marginalization experienced by many people in urban communities! What a challenge to our lifestyles, and what a challenge to do something about it! I picture the rich man sadly turning away and walking off. He clearly loved God deeply, was very committed and had kept all the commandments faithfully for many years. Did he ever change, I wonder?

Jesus strongly identified with marginalized communities: he had a special place in his heart for 'the least of these'—a bias toward the poor. He did not come for the rich, those who had 'made it', but for those who had nothing and knew they had nothing and were therefore open to him. At the heart of this group are the children.

PART TWO

Building: cement and bricks

Meet Sam

Sam—either Samantha or Samuel—is the child who has been born and has grown up in the urban context described above. Our inner cities and outer urban estates are full of children with boundless energy, amazing creativity and a real zest for life. They are also children whose spirituality has been damaged to a greater or lesser degree. These are children who come to our kids' clubs on a regular basis or maybe flit in and out depending on interest, family situations and issues in the peer group.

Here is a picture of Sam, painted for us by the first-hand observations of urban children's workers from a wide variety of contexts.

- spends time on the streets
- low self-esteem
- displays bravado, which can be a mask for lack of confidence
- little respect for authority
- streetwise
- tribal/territorial
- fearless
- mirrors prejudice of parents or close adult figures
- blasé/bored
- competitive
- cool image
- strongly defensive of parents, especially mother
- easily led: peer pressure very strong
- fashion-conscious

- insecure
- restricted
- angry
- short attention span
- needs protection
- thinker
- talented
- no garden
- no private space
- assortment of family backgrounds
- caught between two cultures
- part of an extended family system, or no extended family
- more grown-up or streetwise, but very immature
- representative of a different culture and religion
- non-English-speaking parents
- has more freedom but is less free
- resourceful
- blunt
- aggressive
- risk-taking
- needs attention
- affectionate
- humorous
- loyal: covers for others
- hurting inside
- mischievous
- limited experience of world

Connecting with Sam

How do we even begin to connect with Sam and her world? It may be the case that our own world, including the way we were brought up, is far removed from Sam's in terms of lifestyle and values. Living in the same community can be a start in the right direction, although this is not always possible. More important, as we have already seen, is the quality of the relationship we build with Sam and our attitude towards her, which must be child-centred. The messages Sam has received throughout her life, and the way she has interpreted these messages, will have damaged her spirituality. We want to help her understand some of the affirming things that God has said about her. But Sam has learned that, half the time, adults don't mean what they say, so how are we ever going to help her to hear that God really means it when he says he will be beside her when things get hard? We can say that God is different from the adults she knows, but how is she going to understand that? All she knows about God is as a swear word.

Urban practitioners like to point out that the Bible starts in a garden but ends in a city—a very heartening observation for those of us who thrive in the vibrancy of city life. Then there is 1 Peter 2:4–10, which challenges us to come as living stones to be built up into a temple for the Lord.

Taking these images and thinking about our streetwise urban Sam, who plays in the street and sits on the kerbs (we are appreciative of the association with the acronym CURBS), the CURBS team have borrowed a building analogy—cement and bricks—to illustrate the ways in which we begin to connect with Sam and start to repair and nurture her damaged spirituality. In constructing a building, we first need to prepare our cement and ensure that it is the right consistency. It is crucial to get the cement right because it surrounds all the bricks and holds them firmly in place. What are the bags of cement we need to have ready?

The cement

Start in the child's world

First we need to start in the child's world, not where we think the child ought to be. We need to put aside our agenda and discover what makes the child tick. Some years ago, I undertook a research project in the East London Borough of Newham, looking at the aims of Sunday school teachers in running their groups, and also at the expectations of the children and their reasons for coming to the group. There was little, if any, common ground between the two. The leaders had expectations around the children becoming Christians and/or becoming a part of the church community, whereas the children saw Sunday school primarily as a recreational activity alone. The evidence seemed to suggest that neither group had their aims fulfilled.

Starting in the child's world is also about going to them, not expecting them to come to us. What do they enjoy doing? Whom do they look up to? What issues are around for them? How will things be different next month? This has been a key principle for us in developing the CURBS resources. We have sought to identify and start with the issues that are significant in the child's world: self-esteem, wanting to be first, being cool, unfairness, image and identity, having the biggest and best, being loud-mouthed, handling anger and hatred, to name but a few.

Then we have explored these issues through activities that link with their daily lives. The Christian teaching does not come as a single activity—a 'God slot'—so that we have the 'fun bit' and then comes the 'religious bit'. Children are more integrated (as we discovered above), so, if we are starting in their world, we also need to be integrated. Biblical teaching flows through every activity, every game—including through the way we are and the way we do the game or activity—perhaps explicitly, perhaps implicitly.

Children need to discover that, in the same way, our faith flows through every aspect of our life, spoken or unspoken. We want the children to experience that the 'Christian' bit is not just when we're talking about the Bible, reading it or praying, but that it kicks in at the shops, in the playground, and at home. The Christian faith we are seeking to share is, above all, holistic and relevant.

Earn the right to be heard

Secondly, we need to earn the right to be heard. Adults can be very arrogant, and Christian adults can be the most arrogant of all in assuming that what we have to say, because it is so important (and because we are adults), automatically has a right to be heard. But we have no right to make such assumptions. We need to work slowly and respectfully with children, building their confidence and earning their respect and trust. We need to accord children the same regard that we would adults. Why is it, for example, that we tell children not to interrupt us, but we are quite happy to interrupt a group because we need to speak to a leader? Why do we speak to children in a manner that we would not tolerate if it was them speaking to us? Earning the right to be heard is about valuing children's intrinsic worth.

Be alongside the child

We need to be alongside the child—by the child's side, figuratively speaking. This is a very unique place to be as children's workers. It is not about being ahead: a child has plenty of authority figures in life, like parents and teachers. It is not about being behind, struggling to be heard—although sometimes it feels like that! Being alongside means that our relationship is at the heart of all we do together. We offer the child three gifts in this: the gift of being valued, the gift of being listened to non-judgmentally, and the gift of being accepted unconditionally. What might this mean in practice?

Valuing a child means that we accept and respect a child's comments. We do not ridicule them, no matter how 'off the mark' or out of order they might be, and we make an appropriate response, so that the child realizes if his comment was inappropriate but he himself does not feel devalued or put down. When Mark prayed that Andrew might not be so fat and Andrew burst into tears, we didn't point out that Mark was also plump, but instead tried to help him to see how he was hurting Andrew. We also value a child's work or contribution, no matter what the standard. Just because Tasha produces a better greeting card than Lynn, it doesn't mean that we praise it more highly.

We believe a child and accept the validity of her feelings. When my daughter, in the example cited on page 96, became frightened at separating from us, we didn't tell her not to be so silly, to snap out of it, or to be glad she had got grandparents to look after her. We believed what she was saying and feeling, and we did something about it.

We allow children opportunities to make choices within their capabilities, and in doing so give them permission to make choices that are different from ours, and to make wrong choices. However, we also give them guidance and surround them with safety in case their choices go wrong. We do not focus on the child's powerlessness, but give him the confidence that he has value in and of himself. Valuing the child gives her the message, 'I am of value and what I have to offer is valued. I also have an important contribution to make to the world.'

Listening to children is about affording them recognition, thus meeting their deep hunger for acknowledgment of their existence. Listening non-judgmentally is about accepting what they say, although we may not agree with it. Our response is not to be critical or to jump down their throats, but to help them to see another way of looking at the issue, or another way of responding to a person. Quality listening means that we give the child our full attention, kneeling down to communicate on an equal level if necessary. It means maintaining eye contact, not having our gaze continually flickering off in other directions. Quality listening gives the child the message, 'My knowledge and opinions are worth listening to and have validity, even as a child.'

Accepting a child unconditionally means that we do not confuse 'you are valuable' with 'well done': we do not confuse the child (who is always acceptable to us) with the action (which may not be at all acceptable). We do not favour one child over another; we do not favour the child who conforms to our way of life. It may be

126

tempting to favour Caroline, who is laid back, easygoing and always ready to join in with activities, over Zoë, for whom everything is 'boring', who turns her back on every suggestion you make and sabotages activities when she does join in. Unconditional accept-ance means that we suspend our natural inclination to continually judge and criticize the child who is the hardest to handle, who finds it most difficult to conform. It gives the child the message, 'Even when I play up and don't follow their rules, I might get into trouble, but they still accept me and they will always have me back.'

In these three 'gifts'—valuing, listening and accepting—we give the child the experience of being truly 'seen' for who he or she is. Many of our children have no other opportunity of experiencing this type of quality relationship with an adult.

Build foundations

All we do is about building foundations. This is a slow, long-term task. I believe that the ideal in working with children is to build a long-term relationship over many years, but the reality is that the child moves or we move on. I am encouraged by the realization that Jesus only spent three years in his actual teaching ministry, but they were three crucial years. The key is that he trained up twelve others to continue his ministry. Are we effective in training and resourcing others to continue our work? Or does everything grind to a halt and stop functioning when we leave?

Building foundations is also about recognizing that we are only part of a much larger picture. What we do in our group with Mark may not appear to have any impact: Mark may move on to another area, meet new people and have new experiences. But years ahead, some situation may cause him to remember his relationship with us. Some memory of the way he was treated, the atmosphere of the group, a vague memory of something he learned, combined with new experiences, may eventually bring him to discover for himself what faith is all about. A friend of ours with no Christian back-ground travelled overseas with the Merchant Navy. In the course of his travels, he met someone on board ship who spoke to him about his faith. Our friend stayed in a hotel room and walked off with the Gideon Bible he found in the drawer by his bed. He listened to someone on a soapbox speaking about God: he thought the speaker was cracked, but he listened! Finally, he came back to England, where we regularly used to find him on our doorstep— often under the influence of alcohol, but with many questions about God and the Bible and faith. Eventually it all came together for him and he became a Christian, but all of these experiences in their different ways were foundational to his eventual commitment (see 1 Corinthians 3:6–9).

Work holistically

We need to remember that the child is part of many other systems: the home, the school, the peer group and the community. We may sometimes feel discouraged that we only touch the child for an hour or two, once a week. What difference can that make? We need to remember first of all that it is the quality of our relationship with the child that is all-important. Even an hour can demonstrate to a child what it means to be really valued. Then we need to take on board the value of working holistically. How can we also have an impact on these other systems and so touch the child's world at other levels? Perhaps our time is limited, but surely we can get to know the family networks. Aren't we ourselves part of the same community (unless we live elsewhere)? What are we doing as a Christian member of that community?

The bricks

With these bags of cement ready, it is time to start building. What bricks do we need to put into place in order to effectively repair and nurture a child's spirituality?

The foundation stone

Returning again to 1 Corinthians 3, we see that the foundation stone is Christ himself. If we want our building to last, then we need the right foundation: 'God has already placed Jesus Christ as the one and only foundation, and no other foundation can be laid' (1 Corinthians 3:11, GNB). Our aim in CURBS is simple: however you phrase it, it is to help children on their journey in the kingdom of God by being alongside them, teaching them and learning from them.

The first level

Once we have set in place the true foundation of our work, we are in a position to recognize our key role as children's workers. We may have carefully selected the best resources; we may have spent time thinking about the 'bricks' we hope to put in place; but the child's first point of contact is with us. We are the screen, if you like, through which all that the child experiences in the group is mediated. So, in a sense, we are the first 'brick' to be put in place as we seek to rebuild the child's damaged spirituality.

We have already seen the importance of relationships within the 'healthy village' and of the 'enlightened witness' who is there for the child. How many of us can remember one particular person as we grew up who was an important role model for us? Too often, our highly individualistic Western culture gives us the message that we should be able to manage on our own, that it is a sign of weakness to ask for help. From childhood we receive an unspoken message that it is a sign of strength to learn to do things on our own. Boarding schools are a good illustration of this. Never mind that the child is sent away from his family to a strange environment, with unfamiliar rules and different expectations. Never mind that he may be homesick and miserable. 'They're all like this at the beginning,' comes the response. 'It will pass. It will make a man of him!' Of course it will pass because, as the child discovers that he is left to manage on his own, he learns to shut down his needs and to develop coping strategies in order to survive.

Recent research has shown that children learn best in the context of supportive relationships, whether adult or peer. The work of the Russian psychologist Lev Vygotsky indicates that a greater emphasis needs to be placed on the social dimension—the relationship with others—in the process of learning and development. His approach stresses the role of social interaction as key to the child's developing understanding. He suggests that the optimum setting for learning is in a relationship with another, where the other person, either an adult or a peer, can 'scaffold' the child's learning, enabling him or her through the relationship to accomplish the given task and progress to the next.

The image of scaffolding is very helpful. Picture a new office block being built. As the structure grows higher and higher, so the scaffolding rises alongside. The scaffolding is there to support the building and also to enable it to rise higher, because if there is no scaffold set up around the building, no one can reach the top of the building to add more bricks. The kids we work with are the building, and we are the scaffolding. We are there to support them (in areas where they might not otherwise be supported) and we are there to enable them to grow and develop even more. Through our relationship with them, they are enabled to experience and discover new things. What a privilege for us!

Fresh perspectives

An openness to see things from fresh perspectives is crucial when working with a child's spirituality. I much prefer working alongside churches and groups in inner cities or on outer urban estates. My experience has been that when churches are struggling, it is then that they will look for new approaches, new ideas, or new ways of *being* church. They are challenged to look at the essentials because, if they don't, they may die. When numbers are strong, however, churches only look for new ways of *doing* things, which can be a superficial approach. High numbers can sometimes lead to complacency and mask the need to revisit essentials.

Fresh perspectives can involve putting all aspects of our children's work on the table and re-evaluating them. It is a good idea to do this periodically, even if our groups are going well, as it can prevent us from becoming complacent and it can challenge us to see if there is anything we could be doing more effectively. Too often, we only stop to take stock when things are not going well—for example, if numbers are low or we have a leadership crisis. Re-assessing the situation on a regular basis may help to prevent such crises.

Perhaps we need to think about the profile of children's work within our church as a whole. Are we in a community where there are lots of children? Is reaching them one of the mission priorities of the church? If so, why not challenge the church leadership to designate one month as a children's month, with services, sermons, talks, midweek activities and community activities all focused around raising the profile of children's work in the church? Make it a month to recommission leaders, recruit new leaders, contact new children, and re-evaluate the timing, extent and content of the children's work. But don't lose the energy after that month. Continue by giving the church regular monthly updates as to how the work is progressing, including snippets in the notices or church newsletter, short presentations by the children, and invitations to visit or view activities.

Ask questions. Do we need more leaders? Do we need helpers—those who may not be involved in actually running the groups, but are there as support, helping to set up, provide snacks, or be a listening ear for the kids? What sort of training does each group need? Who provides it and where can we get it?

Do we involve the children in decisions that are taken regarding them and their activities? Is our timing of children's activities right? Are numbers really low on a Sunday? Do we need to abandon traditional Sunday school and put all our energies into one good midweek activity? Are churched and unchurched kids good at mixing, or is it best to run two separate groups? What about content?

Are we tired ourselves of the resources we've been using? If so, the kids will certainly pick this up! What about some new approaches? Have we explored, for example, the Godly Play approach?[2] Would this suit one group but not another?

What are our aims in our children's work? Are they about evangelism, education or nurture? Are they about all three, but in different groups? Are we trying to achieve two or more aims in the one group? What issues does this raise? Have we ever sat down as a children's work team and set out our objectives together as leaders —and with the children? What qualities do we really want to see develop in our children? An article in the *International Journal of Children's Spirituality*[3] suggested that, when referring to spiritual understanding, schools are speaking of developing the following qualities in their students:

- self-esteem
- relationships with others
- their own personal beliefs
- their own personal values
- appreciation of the beliefs and values of others
- a sense of awe, mystery and wonder
- individual creativity
- an awareness of the fundamental questions of life
- reflection on the meaning and purpose of life
- appropriate responses to life's challenging experiences

What a challenge to us in our churches to set similar goals with regard to our children! Do we even begin to look at our children from this perspective? The children's work team from one church in North London has given serious thought to what they hope to achieve in their work, and has come up with the following aims:

- to establish relationships of trust with the children by being there/being consistent
- to model different ways of behaving

- to allow the children space to express themselves and their needs in a place without burdens, where they can rest and be children
- to allow the parents some space and to take some stress off the family unit
- to show the children that they are loved and valued as individuals created by God
- to allow the children the opportunity to talk about God and to meet with him
- to allow the children to achieve

The children and families who have the privilege to be a part of the children's ministry at that church are indeed blessed.

In short, a willingness to explore new perspectives means that there is nothing that cannot be looked at critically. It may mean deciding that no changes are needed. It may be that you make a few or many changes. What is important is the openness to be challenged and the willingness to make changes.

The child's own world

Understanding the importance of engaging with the child's own world and experiences is a key building block in repairing damaged spirituality. We have already looked at this from our perspective as leaders—the importance of not starting with our agenda. If we look at it from the perspective of the children, we need to realize that it is the messages children have absorbed in growing up, and the experiences they have had, that have caused the damage. Therefore, we need to enter the world of the child in order to begin to repair the damage.

We start with the world the child knows—a world of friendships, loneliness, competition, self-image, self-worth, fun, family problems, fear, peer pressure, death and loss—and use these issues as springboards for exploration and questions. We start in a world that does not make assumptions about children's knowledge of the Bible, about their interest or ability in reading, about their family backgrounds and values, or about the types of activities they are exposed to at home, in the street or at school. We explore what is current for the kids. We do all we can to make real contact with them.

We do not engage as Christian to non-Christian, because this means seeing the child as an object, and our meeting is centred around an agenda: the child becoming a Christian. Instead we engage as person to person, because this means respecting the child as an individual. In this real contact the child cannot help but sense that we value the child for who he or she is. This begins to repair the child's spirituality, and, in the quality of the contact, he or she will be enabled to see Jesus Christ in us because our faith is at the core of our being.

Once we have engaged genuinely with the child's own world, then we have earned the right to cross the bridge and say, 'And in the Bible there is a similar situation…'; 'I know a story of someone who also faced that issue…'; 'I know someone I have found who has really helped me…'; 'Jesus told a story here about someone else who couldn't find an answer…'; ' There's someone here in the Psalms who felt just as angry at God as you do…' and so on.

Our cultural bias

When we work with children in an urban context, and in particular in a multi-cultural urban context, we need to be aware of our own cultural bias: we need to be aware of where we are coming from. Are our expectations of children derived from our own upbringing? For example, do we expect them to attend regularly, sit still and be quiet, or use the right words? What behaviours are culturally bound and which are to do with a more universal respect and courtesy towards one another? What are the expectations of children in schools?

Many children are used to a soundbite culture in which images and content change rapidly, on television or on videos. Many children are used to multi-tasking: watching television, listening to the radio, doing homework, eating and texting. How do we find ways of introducing space and stillness into their busy worlds?

How do we support children struggling to make sense of growing up in two cultures? Have we sufficiently examined our own attitudes toward other faiths to respond openly and respectfully to the families of children who come to us from other faith communities? What are our prejudices, our biases? Do these colour our response to the children?

Our familiarity with scripture

I was privileged to grow up in a Christian family, but I have often felt that I missed out on experiencing what it must be like to encounter the Bible, its stories and characters, for the first time. Instead, they have always been a part of my story, either in the forefront or often—perhaps unfortunately—as a comforting blanket in the background.

We need to be aware of our own familiarity with scripture at several levels. First, we need to ensure that we don't take for granted that children know the Bible stories, even ones as familiar to us as the Christmas story. For many of our children, this will be completely new, or they may have a garbled version of the story, which owes more to Christmas songs and television programmes than to the Bible. I recall doing an activity with a group of nine- and ten-year-olds, which involved sorting Christmas cards into piles depending on the story illustrated—for example, the wise men, the shepherds and the holy family. The children were at a loss with some of the pictures, simply because they had no idea which bit of which story was being depicted: 'Were these presents given by those blokes on the camels or these shepherds?' Related to this, we need to avoid using Christian 'jargon' or terminology. It may be a short cut for us to express something, but it can be meaningless to the kids. We have all heard the apocryphal stories of children saying, 'Our Father who's Martin Evans' or singing, 'I will make you vicious old men'! It is a challenge to us, also, to rephrase words or concepts like 'prayer', 'being saved', 'peace', even 'Creator of the world'.

We also need to remember that children are not 'jugs to be filled' but 'flames to be fanned'. We are not about simply educating the children to know the Bible, in the sense of telling them story after story, quizzing them as to how well they remember, and giving a new memory verse to learn each week. The children are not empty jugs needing to be filled with knowledge, important as the knowledge may be. This approach can be not unlike school, and will therefore give a negative message to children who are alienated from the school system, or who long to do well but for whom this approach to learning is a turn-off. It can damage an already fragile sense of self-worth. Rather, we want to fan the flame of spirituality that is already there in the child.

In experiencing the stories and exploring the verses together, we choose themes and passages that will touch the child and that he will be able to relate to in a meaningful way. So we will not tell the story of Noah and the ark just because it is about animals and lends itself to some good craft activities. We will think about whether the theme of God's judgment and anger with evil, and his justice, will be meaningful to the world of our six-year-old or eleven-year-old. The story of David fighting the giant Goliath may be a great story for eight-year-old boys, but let's start in their world. Does it have something to say that the boys can relate to? What does the parable of the vineyard owner who employed people at the end of the day for the same rate as those at the beginning of the day say to kids who have a very strong sense of fairness? Are children in a place to move past that, to grasp the truth that God treats us all equally?

What we need to ask is, 'How does the gospel look, feel or sound from the child's perspective?' What does it have to say to a world of estate living, multi-cultural experiences, stranger danger, pop music, computer chat rooms, reconstituted families, and all the many issues that engage a child's attention every day? The challenge to us is to put aside our own familiarity with the Bible and to rediscover new truths in well-known stories. We look at the gospel through the child's eyes and from her perspective and find new meaning in the stories. This surely is part of what it means to learn from a child.

Experience and awareness

In an urban context, we often work with children who are alienated from a school system where the predominant emphasis is on cognitive learning. I spent some time assisting in a Year 6 class in our local primary school. 'These children do not need the literacy hour and the numeracy hour,' commented the teacher one day. 'We need to get rid of the desks, put bean bags in their place, and let the children come and unload all the baggage they are carrying from home.' In fact, were the school system to allow it (which it cannot, because of the demands of the National Curriculum), there are many ways of teaching that can touch the affective side of the child and create a context for the necessary learning to take place, at the same time as offering space for the child to offload. We can do a small part of this within our groups, but we need to be absolutely convinced ourselves that experience and awareness are more important than simply learning facts and figures.

Going back to the story of the sermon about the loving father, referred to on pages 14–15, perhaps you will act the story out and end the session with a celebratory party. Maybe the child who played the part of the lost son rarely experiences a party that celebrates him for who he is. It may be a moment of sheer delight for him. Perhaps he won't remember the facts of the story—the significance of the son feeling sorry and returning home. However, his experience of the party, and his awareness that for some reason it was celebrating him, may remain with him for a long time.

In our sessions, we need to use ways of creative expression that touch the child's spirituality. Go back to the outline of what constitutes a child's spirituality on pages 28–36. We need consciously to think about approaches that will nurture and reawaken children's openness to the world around them, to feelings, to people; their ability to live in the present, their spontaneity and their imagination.

Take a critical look, for example, at your surroundings. How can you help children to celebrate the world around? Divide them into groups, each with a disposable camera. Give them a route and a shopping list of photos to take, items to collect and activities to do, like brick rubbings. Come back and have each group create a display. Kids may hear their urban communities rubbished, but look at what they've discovered—so much to be proud of!

Tell a story in a creative way, using puppets, drama and craft; then have the children draw faces that show how they felt, or how the characters might have felt at given points. Why do they think the characters felt like this? Do they themselves ever feel the same way?

Take a trip out to the country or the beach. Look together at a night sky or at an endless horizon, or simply at so much water. Many city kids never experience such space, such darkness, or so many stars. Engage their imagination through story, through music, through various art forms. Recognize that children learn in different ways and what may be good for some may be 'naff' to others, so provide different options, remembering that attention spans are short.

All of these creative approaches can be easily linked into our children's groups, whether they are Sunday groups, midweek activities or holiday clubs. But they will involve a rethink on our part, until our child-centred attitude is firmly in place and we learn to look at each activity, each biblical story and element of teaching from the child's perspective, thinking, 'What do my group need at the moment? How can my approaches to this story or activity nurture the children's spirituality? What particular aspects of their spirituality need to be reawakened?'

Measurement

There is a real 'down side' to this entire approach of nurturing the child's spirituality, which I believe is why so few of us consistently attempt it. How do you measure your progress? How can you be sure that progress is even happening? In a culture that looks for outcomes and measures success by league tables, the reality is that engaging with a child's spirituality is far less measurable than the transfer of facts.

We as leaders are products of the 'outcome culture', so in order for us to feel that we are achieving something, we need to be able to tick the boxes and see that we have completed our agenda. If a child has learned a memory verse and can remember it the following week, that is a box we can tick. But the more important question is: has the child really taken on board what the verse means? Most people can remember words, but how can you know if the truth of the verse has become a part of the child? The simple answer is, you can't: you cannot measure that. But from what we know of children, it is far more likely that the verse will mean something if, beyond simply learning and repeating the words, the verse has been illustrated in such a way as to touch their affective side—their spirituality—whether through story, through drama, through relating it to personal experience, or through art. Educational theory teaches us that simply 'telling it' does not mean the message is communicated. Children remember 90 per cent of what they do, but only ten per cent of what they hear. As children's workers, we are very good at the telling; let's explore the affective side of 'doing'.

There is another side to this coin, however: our understanding of children as set out in this book teaches us that their spirituality needs nurturing, that the image of God in each child needs to be touched, nurtured, and reawakened where it is disappearing. Therefore we can know that, if we are following these principles, progress is being made. Above all, the one aspect that we can measure (or perhaps 'monitor' is a better word) is the quality of our relationship with the child. As we have seen, the most effective way of communicating with children is by becoming incarnate, coming alongside them in their world and making it our world, which involves high-cost commitment. This, after all, is at the heart of all we do.

In conclusion

As we try to develop and nurture our children's spirituality, we are doing a number of things. First, we are recognizing and valuing the spirituality that is already there within the child. We are affirming and celebrating the truth that each child is made in God's image. Second, we are offering children the opportunity to work with issues such as their imagination, their feelings, their creativity, their longing for recognition and for being valued, and their longing to be listened to and accepted unconditionally. We are making these qualities acceptable in a world that so often tells them otherwise. Third, we are helping to give children a language and a way of expressing these experiences. Within our churches, this is opening up access to ideas and truths that are specifically Christian. Finally, through it all, we are providing a 'springboard to faith', giving children the means whereby they can enter into and engage with Christian values and with the Bible. In doing so, we are reversing the trend of a secularized society, which either rubbishes such experiences or—as is so often the case in urban communities—boxes them into a privatized spirituality. Instead, we are celebrating them. We believe that to have such experiences is what it means to be made in the image of God and to be in real relationship with others and ultimately with God in Christ Jesus.

NOTES

1 The material describing the urban context is part of a CURBS training module, much of which was devised by Liz Dorton, a member of the CURBS Resource and Training Teams.
2 See Jerome W. Berryman, *Godly Play: An Imaginative Approach to Religious Education* (Augsburg, 1995) or visit www.godlyplay.co.uk.
3 Geriant Davies, 'What is Spiritual Development? Primary Headteachers' Views' in *International Journal of Children's Spirituality*, Volume 3, Number 2, December 1998, p. 134.

The story continues

One hundred years from now…
it will not matter what my bank account was,
the sort of house I lived in,
or the kind of car I drove,
but
the world may be different
because
I was important in the life of a child.[1]

So you've read the book. That's the easy part. We've all read books, closed them up and said, 'There's some useful ideas there—I must do something about them.' But our good intentions have disappeared under busy schedules. The question we need to ask is, 'Do I really want something to change in our church's work with our neighbourhood kids? Am I going to take the steps to see that this happens?'

Let's look at some practical ways in which we can start to implement the ideas in this book.

Gather a team

Doing children's work in a small, under-resourced urban church can be very lonely work. Coordinating the children's work—Sunday activities, midweek clubs, parent and toddler groups, crèche or whatever it might be—often falls in the lap of one or two leaders. These leaders may well have nine-to-five jobs and kids of their own;

they may be elderly and retired; they may be single mums, already overstretched; or one of them may be the minister's wife—and it's not easy to keep a sense of freshness, energy and commitment week after week. You may be thinking, 'Sure, the ideas in this book are great, but get real: I practically have to pay someone from the church just to come and sit in a corner and smile so that I can meet the requirements of the Children Act.' Don't worry: that very thought has already been expressed by a highly committed children's worker!

I know what it's like. I've been there, and I'm convinced that the answer is to create a team. But from where? Well, start with the few people in your own church. It will take time, but meet maybe once a month to pray for your kids, their families and your groups, to plan for the next month, to brainstorm new ideas, and to share frustrations and disappointments. I can hear you already: 'Recruitment is our biggest problem.' You are not alone: this seems to be one of the biggest issues facing our children's work today. Find out why it is so in your church.

Is it time? Try recruiting for a four- or six-week block: often leaders don't come forward because they feel that they're signing their life away in children's work. A short commitment is manageable and gives folk the opportunity just to dip their toe in the water. Who knows—they might really enjoy it and volunteer for more.

Is it fear? 'I could never do that—I'm hopeless with kids.' Is it lack of experience? Set up a taster session to show what's involved, then follow with some training sessions. Evenings might be easiest, or Saturday mornings or afternoons, leaving folk time to do their shopping. Help people to see what's involved, to share their concerns and develop the confidence that they could do it and that they don't need to be frightened off by the idea.

Is it conflict of teaching styles? Do you have teachers who have taught for years in the same way and find it hard to adapt to a different approach? First take time to sit down together and look at how children are different today from when they started teaching. Listen to their views and share yours. Bring in some of the insights from this book about children, their families and the messages with which they grow up. (It's a lot easier when someone else says it as well!) Most old-style teachers have a real heart for the children and will be genuinely concerned to explore ways to reach them, provided you involve them and seek to carry them with you.

Another aspect of recruitment is that we often wait for someone to volunteer for children's work. Why not pray specifically that God will show you the person of his choice? Then go and ask them. It may be someone who has never worked with children and who would never have considered it. God can surprise us—and them!

If none of this is possible for whatever reason—or even if it is possible and you want to make it better—go and knock on the doors of children's workers in neighbouring churches who face similar issues to yours. Meeting to share frustrations and encouragements and to pray together is an incredibly supportive experience. So much can come out of it in terms of new ideas for your own group as well as for joint activities. And don't meet on church premises: meet in someone's house with some food and drink. You might even want to look together at some of the principles in this book—the hungers, for example, on pages 39–52—and apply them to your own situations and your own kids. What new insights can you gain that will enrich your ministry?

I am always struck by Jesus' example. He didn't go it alone. Everywhere he went, everything he did was with members of his team, and I don't believe that this was only so that he could teach them. He also needed them. Gethsemane is a good example of this—although his little team let him down. We need a team to work with. If you simply can't see how this can happen, start praying with your eyes open and see where God is starting to do things.

Create a healthy village

You thought creating a team was a challenge, but that's nothing compared with this! Creating a healthy village is about nothing less than getting your whole church to become aware of and to re-evaluate its approach to the children and families in its midst and surrounding it. First of all, be relieved: your job is to lay a few bricks, not to turn the whole church around in six months. In fact, turning your church into a 'healthy village' is a very long-term project, and it may be that there are far too many issues around (way beyond your responsibility to deal with) that prevent it ever becoming one. But you must be faithful in laying the bricks. Get your newly created team together to brainstorm what bricks might be appropriate to your individual churches. Maybe in some areas you could build jointly. Here are a few ideas as starters.

Raise the profile of your children's work among the congregation. Quite often, lack of support isn't lack of interest. It may simply be ignorance, busyness or apathy. Do folk know what children's work is actually going on? Do they know what sorts of activities you do? Have you ever specifically told them? Lots of people ignore notices that don't apply to them. Do they know any of the kids? Keep folk updated, with regular children's work slots in your service. Don't make them part of your notices: the notices are usually boring and folk will fall asleep through them. Instead, make them a feature in their own right. Give out a little A5 leaflet periodically to accompany your news: the children could design and write it. Have the kids make a small presentation. Give each person a sticker or badge to wear that says, 'I support (or I pray for) the children's work (or the name of the activity) at my church.' Challenge them to wear it all week. Get folk to collect for or contribute to things you need—and tell them what you need. Encourage prayer for each of your children. Invite people to miss church and drop in on what you're doing with the kids.

Your team will come up with lots of other ideas.

Start work on your minister. Point out to him/her some of the things Jesus said and did around kids. Give him/her this book to read if necessary. Ask for a series of sermons around the statements Jesus made about children (for example, 'become like a child' or 'their angels have constant access to the Father'), and the implications for us as Christians and for our work with children. Don't be surprised if your minister is not too keen, or if you need to lend him/her some books. After all, input on the biblical approach to children, a children's hermeneutic, children's spirituality, and even children's work in general hardly feature at all in any theological training (with a few exceptions). You could gently encourage your minister to read a few of the books suggested in the guide to further reading at the end of this book.

Suggest that the minister's talks are in the context of a month (or some such period) of raising the profile of children's work in the church. This could include a general raising of awareness of the challenges of children's work in the church: the need for more leaders, the need for training, the need for the church to be more child-friendly, the need to develop a child-centred attitude, and so on. As part of the profile-raising, ensure that there is a service of commissioning and/or recommissioning of children's workers on a regular basis. Try to find a couple of members of the congregation who will commit themselves to pray regularly for each person in the children's work team throughout the year. You need this kind of prayer support in this kind of mission.

Help the church to become more child-aware. A 'healthy village' offers children enough support to help them develop in healthy directions. Part of this support is enabling the adults at church to really learn to 'see' children. Some adults feel uncomfortable around children, some fear them (especially groups of them) and some see them just as nuisances and troublemakers. Let's face it, you are never going to get everyone to appreciate children in the way you do, but that doesn't mean you do nothing.

Do you have home groups at your church? How about a short series on understanding children, beginning with how Jesus sees children? If that's not possible, try a three-minute slot in the service each Sunday, entitled, 'Have you ever thought...?' Have you ever thought... about Jesus' attitude to children? Have you ever thought... why it is important to speak to a child by name?

Have you ever thought… why kids can't sit still in a service? Have you ever thought… why Sam (don't use a real child's name) might be so quiet around adults? Have you ever thought… that in welcoming a child, we're welcoming Jesus? Have you ever thought… how hard it must be for Nadia to grow up between two cultures? Have you ever thought… why we put so much effort into our work with under-sevens? Take some of the ideas from this book that have struck you, and get your team to help you distil them into questions. Afterwards, collate them into a 'Have you ever thought…?' booklet that you can give to new folk who come to the church, to help them see how much you value children. A child who is really 'seen' for who he or she is, rather than just glanced at superficially, is a child who will feel valued, affirmed and accepted. What a gift for our churches to give a child!

Help the church to become more family-aware. There are always those in the church who say loud and clear, 'I blame the parents!' You may need to do a slot entitled, 'Have you ever thought… of the pressures on a parent?' Folk in the church need to appreciate that the parents and families of many of the children who come to our groups are in desperate need of support, help and encouragement themselves. Explore as a church how you can help them. Are they isolated? Do they find that it demands too much energy to take out three kids under five? Are they finding it hard to cope with their kids' behaviour? Is language a barrier? Do they need a listening ear or a shoulder to cry on? How about a coffee morning for carers and kids? This could be a team venture, as you may not have anyone free during the day at your church. How about babysitting the kids for an evening to give Mum or the parents some space? What about parenting classes, or language classes? Could some members of your team do home visits? A home visit doesn't have to be heavy. It can simply be ten minutes to say 'hello' or tell the parents that this or that activity is happening and you thought they might like to come. Alternatively, a phone call can do the same thing, take less time and be less intrusive, although it is less personal.

Another possibility might be a family weekend at the church, with activities to suit all tastes. If you have lots of 'fringe' families and individuals and you want to build relationships, try doing what a small church of 30–40 people did in East London and book up a week at Butlins for church folk, friends and neighbours—no strings attached. They had over 70 adults and children join them.

Finally, remember that a healthy village is one that includes support for the child's wider setting. Who or what else is a part of your children's setting? The school is often a key aspect. What links do you have with local schools? Can your minister or your team get involved in helping with assemblies, with aspects of the religious education syllabus or PSHE (Personal, Social and Health Education)? Do you have premises (for example, a large hall) that the school might like to use for some activities? Do you have church members or parents who are involved as teachers or lunchtime supervisors, or who go into the school to hear children read, and so on? Ask them what sort of support you can offer as a church.

What about within the neighbourhood—local shops, play areas, busy roads? Are there issues of safety, security or needed facilities with which you could get involved, which ultimately would improve the quality of life of your children and the community as a whole?

Ah yes, the children!

We come to the children last because you have done so much already in terms of setting in place the context within which your children's work can flourish. Offering to your children the experience of being a part of a 'healthy village' is a rare gift indeed.

We've already seen that at the heart of all you do with your children is the quality of your relationship with them. Activities, resources and holiday clubs are all secondary to this. But a relationship doesn't just happen—it has to be worked at. What does this involve? Here are a few practical ideas.

Get to know the families—parents, brothers, sisters, grandparents, or other key carers. Find out where they live, and visit them. Some members of your team will undoubtedly know some of the families from other contexts, as you will already have some links. But don't miss out other families or those who only turn up occasionally. To begin with, it may be a quick doorstep stop to invite them to appropriate activities at the church. Maybe they won't come initially, but don't give up. Don't have any ulterior motive: just be a friend and offer some time to the family. Based on what you have gleaned from your visits, you may want to consider wider church involvement in the types of activities that would be welcomed, such as a coffee morning, help with gardening or minor house repairs, language classes, debt counselling, help with moving furniture, and so on. Again, it will take time, but families will respond if they see that you are there for them and their children, rather than simply interested in getting them into church.

Knowing the family will help you to understand the messages the kids have received in their growing up and the issues they bring to your groups. You will be able to identify areas where your children would benefit from input: for example, ways of building their self-esteem, ways to help them structure their time, or appropriate ways of contact, both physical and verbal. You may realize that your children are lacking in opportunities for stimulating activities, that they need their horizons broadened at all sorts of levels. You may be able to identify certain behaviours as coping strategies developed by children, which hide a need that they are no longer able to voice or have disowned. So much can come from a quality relationship.

The challenge then is to help them to experience God's love within this setting—to help them make the important connections between their stories and God's story. When they feel heard and understood by you and have experienced your being there for them, then they will be open to hearing and experiencing God's love, mediated through you and the resources you use. A belief in the importance of building quality relationships lies at the heart of all the resources that have been produced by the CURBS team.

Each CURBStone Kit endeavours to suggest activities that involve opportunities for relationship building. The team takes as a starting point issues that are relevant to the children's own world, and builds the kits from the ground up. We try our best to listen to where the children are coming from and then, having earned the right to be heard, we help them discover what the Bible says that can speak into their situation.

Continuing the story

This book is rather like a station on a train journey. I've stopped here temporarily and written down an account of where I started, who I've met and what I've seen on the journey so far. By the next station, I will have met more people and discovered a lot more new insights. What I write then, although enriched by what I have already experienced, will be different again. Those of us in CURBS do not see ourselves in any way as 'experts' in children's work. We are simply practitioners who have been faced with a need and have tried to respond to the need in the best way we can. We have, perhaps, had the privilege of more opportunities to reflect on the children we work with and their situations, and to explore new approaches, than many people doing similar work.

However, going back to the idea of working as a team, we believe that CURBS would be enriched by your experiences and insights in working with urban children. So if you have read this book and have found in it some useful ideas, help us to continue the story by becoming partners with us on our journey. Visit our website and e-mail us with your reflections, experiences and insights. Together we may be able to make an even bigger impact on the lives of the children with whom we work and to whom we are so deeply committed.

website: www.curbsproject.org.uk
e-mail: info@curbsproject.org.uk

NOTE

1   Source unknown.

References

Berne, Eric, *What Do You Say After You Say Hello?* (Corgi, 1975)

Berryman, Jerome, *Godly Play: An imaginative Approach to Religious Education* (Augsburg, 1995)

Browne, Anthony, 'Babies socialise within seconds' in *The Observer*, 9 July 2000

Buckland, Ron, *Perspectives on Children and the Gospel* (Scripture Union Australia, 2001)

Bunge, Marcia J., *The Child in Christian Thought* (Eerdmans, 2001)

Cole, Robert, *The Spiritual Life of Children* (HarperCollins, 1992)

DeVries, Dawn, 'Toward a Theology of Childhood' in *Interpretation: A Journal of Bible and Theology*, Vol 55, No 2, April 2001

Dillard, Annie, *An American Childhood* (Harper and Row, 1987)

Hay, David with Nye, Rebecca, *The Spirit of the Child* (HarperCollins, 1998)

Henderson, Stewart, *Homeland* (Hodder & Stoughton, 1993)

Illsley Clarke, Jean, *Self Esteem: A Family Affair* (Hazelden, 1998)

Joseph, Sandra (ed.), Theresa Prout and Anne Hargest Gorzelak (trans.), *A Voice for the Child: The Inspirational Words of Janusz Korczak* (HarperCollins, 1999)

Lapworth, Phil; Sills, Charlotte; and Fish, Sue, *Transactional Analysis Counselling* (Winslow Press, 1993)

Lee, Robert G., 'Ethics: A Gestalt of Values/The Values of Gestalt— A Next Step' in *Gestalt Review 2002*, Vol 6, Number 1

Lee, Robert G. and Wheeler, Gordon, *The Voice of Shame: Silence and*

Connection in Psychotherapy (Jossey-Bass, 1996)

Miles, Glen and Wright, Josephine-Joy, eds., *Celebrating Children: Equipping people working with children and young people living in difficult circumstances around the world* (Paternoster, 2003)

Miller, Alice, *The Drama of Being a Child: The Search for the True Self* (Virago, 2001)

Miller, Alice, *Banished Knowledge* (Virago, 1991)

Mooney, Bel, *Here's Kitty!* (Mammoth, 1992)

Nouwen, Henri, *Gracias! A Latin American Journal* (Orbis Books, 1993)   *i*

Nouwen, Henri, *Walk With Jesus: Stations of the Cross* (Orbis Books, 1990)

Oaklander, Violet, *Windows to Our Children* (Gestalt Journal Press, 1988)

Stern, Daniel, *The Interpersonal World of the Infant: A View from Psychoanalysis and Developmental Psychology* (Basic Books, 1985)

Wheeler, Gordon and McConville, Mark, eds., *The Heart of Development: Gestalt Approaches to Working with Children, Adolescents and their Worlds*, Vol 1: *Childhood* (GestaltPress, 2002)

White, Keith, 'Exploring Child Theology', keynote paper for the Archbishops' Council's Strategy for Children Forum, 10 March 2004

Wickes, Frances G., *The Inner World of Childhood* (Coventure, 1977 edition)

Wiederkehr, Macrina, *A Tree Full of Angels* (HarperCollins,1990)

Wiederkehr, Macrina, *Behold Your Life* (Ave Maria Press, 2000)

Further reading on spirituality and spiritual development

Berryman, Jerome W., *Godly Play* (Augsburg Press, 1991). Adaptation of Montessori approach to children's nurture in church.

Berryman, Jerome W., *Teaching Godly Play* (Abingdon Press, 1995). Developing spirituality through self-discipline and responsibility.

Bradford, John, *Caring for the Whole Child* (Children's Society, 1995). A holistic approach to spirituality.

Bunge, Marcia J., *The Child in Christian Thought* (Eerdmans, 2001). Christian theologians' and leaders' views of children across the centuries.

Cavaletti, Sofia, *The Religious Potential of the Child* (Catechesis of the Good Shepherd Publications, 1992). A biblical and sacramental approach to nurturing children's spirituality.

Coles, Robert, *The Spiritual Life of Children* (HarperCollins, 1992). Looking at children's insights into spirituality through their own eyes.

Hay, David and Nye, Rebecca, *The Spirit of the Child* (Fount, 1998). A summary of the findings of the Children's Spirituality Project.

Hull, John, *God-talk with Young Children* (University of Birmingham and CEM, 1991). Finding ways of helping children to express their spirituality.

Joseph, Sandra (ed.), Theresa Prout and Anne Hargest Gorzelak (trans.), *A Voice for the Child: The Inspirational Words of Janusz Korczak* (HarperCollins, 1999). The insights and wisdom of a doctor, writer, teacher and fighter for the child's rights.

Kimes Myers, Barbara, *Young Children and Spirituality* (Routledge, 1997). Applying spirituality to practical settings, for example, in school.

Pritchard, Gretchen Wolff, *Offering the Gospel to Children* (Cowley, 1992). A liturgical approach to grounding the gospel for children in church.

Stonehouse, Catherine, *Joining Children on the Spiritual Journey* (Baker Books, 1998). How parents and teachers can enhance a child's spiritual development.

155

Where are the Children?

Evangelism beyond Sunday morning

Margaret Withers

Most youngsters who come to church are the children of the adult congregation and, depressingly, nearly half of our churches claim that they have no children at all. If we look beyond Sunday morning, however, we see a more optimistic picture.

There are children worshipping regularly at family services, and attending parent and toddler clubs, midweek activities and church schools. There are children who come to Mothering Sunday, Harvest, Parade or Christingle services. There are children at school carol services, or guests at baptisms or weddings. And there are the hidden children who use the church hall for sports or drama, belong to uniformed organizations or visit a church as part of an RE lesson.

This book is about enabling those children to hear the Christian story. It aims to provide thought-provoking guidance to explore the wealth of opportunities for evangelism among children, and a training base for clergy and children's workers.

Drawing on many years' experience, Margaret Withers:

- reviews the ways we can engage with young people and the obstacles that we unwittingly put in the way
- examines strategic planning and ways of managing change
- explores the rationale for evangelism among children
- provides advice on running specific clubs or activities

ISBN 1 84101 361 7   £7.99
Available from your local Christian bookshop or direct from BRF using the order form on page 159.

Why Siblings Matter

Growing strong relationships in church and community

Anna Brooker

For people of all ages today, life can feel fickle. One day the scene seems happy and secure, the next all security is washed away as unresolved tensions, hurts and differences add to the everyday pressures of life. What do we cling on to at such times—friends, relatives, colleagues, the church?

This book looks at the importance of sibling relationships in our individual lives and in families. It considers how these horizontal relationships can strengthen families as much as the vertical, parent–child relationships can. It also looks at the biblical principles that may be applied to practical issues in order to withstand the external and internal pressures of today's world.

Why Siblings Matter is designed to be read by individuals and groups. Groups could use the book as the basis for a parenting course, home group, reading group, or informal discussion group. The chapters are self-contained, providing material for eight thought-provoking sessions, which move progressively through the different stages of family life and sibling relationships.

ISBN 1 84101 260 2   £7.99
Available from your local Christian bookshop or direct from BRF using the order form on page 159.

ORDER FORM

REF	TITLE	PRICE	QTY	TOTAL
361 7	*Where are the Children?*	£7.99		
260 2	*Why Siblings Matter*	£7.99		

POSTAGE AND PACKING CHARGES

order value	UK	Europe	Surface	Air Mail
£7.00 & under	£1.25	£3.00	£3.50	£5.50
£7.01–£30.00	£2.25	£5.50	£6.50	£10.00
Over £30.00	free	prices on request		

Postage and packing:

Donation:

Total enclosed:

Name _____ Account Number _____

Address _____

_____ Postcode _____

Telephone Number _____ Email _____

Payment by: Cheque ❏ Mastercard ❏ Visa ❏ Postal Order ❏ Switch ❏

Credit card no. ❏❏❏❏ ❏❏❏❏ ❏❏❏❏ ❏❏❏❏   Expires ❏❏ ❏❏

Switch card no. ❏❏❏❏❏❏❏❏❏❏❏❏❏❏❏❏❏❏

Issue no. of Switch card ❏❏❏❏   Expires ❏❏ ❏❏

Signature _____ Date _____

All orders must be accompanied by the appropriate payment.

Please send your completed order form to:
BRF, First Floor, Elsfield Hall, 15–17 Elsfield Way, Oxford OX2 8FG
Tel. 01865 319700 / Fax. 01865 319701 Email: enquiries@brf.org.uk

❏ Please send me further information about BRF publications.

Available from your local Christian bookshop.   BRF is a Registered Charity

barnabas

Resourcing children's work in church and school

Simply go to **www.brf.org.uk** and visit the barnabas pages

BRF is a Registered Charity

A Browse our books and buy online in our **bookshop**.

B In the **forum**, join discussions with friends and experts in children's work. Chat through the problems we all face, issues facing children's workers, where-do-I-find... questions and more.

C **Free** easy-to-use downloadable **ideas** for children's workers and teachers. Ideas include:
   - Getting going with prayer
   - Getting going with drama
   - Getting going with the Bible... and much more!

D In **The Big Picture**, you'll find short fun reports on Barnabas training events, days we've spent in schools and churches, as well as expertise from our authors, and other useful articles.

E In the section on **Godly Play**, you'll find a general introduction and ideas on how to get started with this exciting new approach to Christian education.